CAMBRIDGE LIBRARY COLLECTION

Books of enduring scholarly value

Travel and Exploration

The history of travel writing dates back to the Bible, Caesar, the Vikings and the Crusaders, and its many themes include war, trade, science and recreation. Explorers from Columbus to Cook charted lands not previously visited by Western travellers, and were followed by merchants, missionaries, and colonists, who wrote accounts of their experiences. The development of steam power in the nineteenth century provided opportunities for increasing numbers of 'ordinary' people to travel further, more economically, and more safely, and resulted in great enthusiasm for travel writing among the reading public. Works included in this series range from first-hand descriptions of previously unrecorded places, to literary accounts of the strange habits of foreigners, to examples of the burgeoning numbers of guidebooks produced to satisfy the needs of a new kind of traveller - the tourist.

Narrative of a Voyage to the West Indies and Mexico in the Years 1599–1602

The publications of the Hakluyt Society (founded in 1846) made available edited (and sometimes translated) early accounts of exploration. The first series, which ran from 1847 to 1899, consists of 100 books containing published or previously unpublished works by authors from Christopher Columbus to Sir Francis Drake, and covering voyages to the New World, to China and Japan, to Russia and to Africa and India. The author of this volume, Samuel Champlain, is better known for his writings on Canada and for founding Quebec City. This account of his 1599 journey with his uncle to the West Indies and Mexico, originally intended for Henri IV of France and translated for the series in 1859, had never previously appeared in print. Champlain provides a valuable illustrated report on natural history and social, economic and political conditions of the region in the early colonial period.

T0370686

Cambridge University Press has long been a pioneer in the reissuing of out-of-print titles from its own backlist, producing digital reprints of books that are still sought after by scholars and students but could not be reprinted economically using traditional technology. The Cambridge Library Collection extends this activity to a wider range of books which are still of importance to researchers and professionals, either for the source material they contain, or as landmarks in the history of their academic discipline.

Drawing from the world-renowned collections in the Cambridge University Library, and guided by the advice of experts in each subject area, Cambridge University Press is using state-of-the-art scanning machines in its own Printing House to capture the content of each book selected for inclusion. The files are processed to give a consistently clear, crisp image, and the books finished to the high quality standard for which the Press is recognised around the world. The latest print-on-demand technology ensures that the books will remain available indefinitely, and that orders for single or multiple copies can quickly be supplied.

The Cambridge Library Collection will bring back to life books of enduring scholarly value (including out-of-copyright works originally issued by other publishers) across a wide range of disciplines in the humanities and social sciences and in science and technology.

Narrative of a Voyage to the West Indies and Mexico in the Years 1599–1602

Translated from the Original and Unpublished Manuscript

SAMUEL CHAMPLAIN
EDITED BY ALICE WILMERE
AND NORTON SHAW

CAMBRIDGE
UNIVERSITY PRESS

CAMBRIDGE UNIVERSITY PRESS

Cambridge, New York, Melbourne, Madrid, Cape Town, Singapore,
São Paolo, Delhi, Dubai, Tokyo

Published in the United States of America by Cambridge University Press, New York

www.cambridge.org
Information on this title: www.cambridge.org/9781108013437

© in this compilation Cambridge University Press 2009

This edition first published 1859
This digitally printed version 2009

ISBN 978-1-108-01343-7 Paperback

WORKS ISSUED BY

The Hakluyt Society.

NARRATIVE OF A VOYAGE TO THE
WEST INDIES AND MEXICO.

M.DCCC.LIX.

Il y a beaucoup d'autres faictz dont ilz ne sont pas grand —
car encores quilz soient comme Il y a aussy dans racine —
qui sappelle passans que les Indiens mangoyent en lieu de pany —
Il me croit ne Vica my Dy dans toute estre Fle ey laquelle —
Il y a grande quantité de caurelsons que Roy dict quilz —
Ornent de cuir ce que Ie ne puis asseurer combien que Ilz —
ayo bon pour plusieurs fois Il a catasses asses pointus —
Le corps assez long pour sa grossour assauant vng pied et
Demy et na que deux Iambes qui sont devant la queue
fort pointues mesles de couleurs grise Iaunastres
Le dict caurelson est Icy represente —

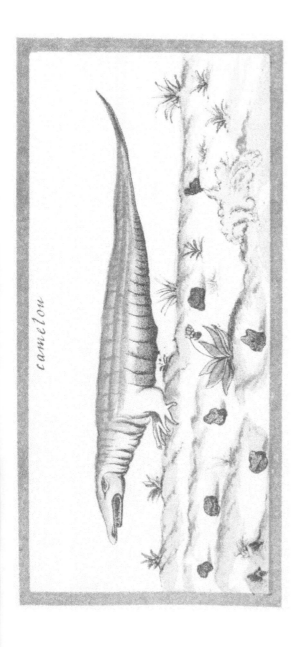

camelon

Les millieurs merchandyse qui sont dans la ý ýle sont
sucres gingambra canifste miel de cannea tabaco
grandtu de cuiva boeufa vaeýea et montone Larý ý eýt

Facsimile of MS

NARRATIVE OF

A VOYAGE

TO THE

WEST INDIES AND MEXICO

IN THE YEARS 1599-1602,

𝔚𝔦𝔱𝔥 𝔐𝔞𝔭𝔰 𝔞𝔫𝔡 𝔍𝔩𝔩𝔲𝔰𝔱𝔯𝔞𝔱𝔦𝔬𝔫𝔰.

BY

SAMUEL CHAMPLAIN.

TRANSLATED FROM THE ORIGINAL AND UNPUBLISHED MANUSCRIPT, WITH A
BIOGRAPHICAL NOTICE AND NOTES BY

ALICE WILMERE.

EDITED BY

NORTON SHAW.

LONDON:
PRINTED FOR THE HAKLUYT SOCIETY.

M.DCCC.LIX.

THE HAKLUYT SOCIETY.

INTRODUCTION.

THE manuscript, of which the following is a translation, as literal as the idioms of the two languages admit, is in the possession of Monsieur Féret, the learned and extremely obliging librarian of the Public Library at Dieppe. Of its originality and authenticity there can be no doubt; the internal evidence of similarity in style, diction, and orthography even, with the published account of Champlain's *Voyages in New France*, would alone suffice to establish those points.[1]

[1] Extract from " Histoire et Description Générale de la Nouvelle France, avec le Journal Historique d'un Voyage fait par ordre du Roi dans l'Amérique Septentrionnale. Par le P. De Charlevoix, de la Compagnie de Jesus." Tome Premier, 12o., Paris, 1744, p. 172. "Le Commandeur de CHATTE, governeur de Dieppe, lui succéda, forma une Compagnie de Marchands de Roüen, avec lesquels plusieurs Personnes de condition entrerent en société, et fit un Armement, dont il confia la conduite à Pontgravé, à qui le Roy avoit donné des Lettres Patentes, pour continuer les découvertes dans le Fleuve du Canada, et pour y faire des Etablissemens. Dans le même tems Samuël de CHAMPLAIN, Gentilhomme Saintongeois, Capitaine de Vaisseau, et en réputation d'Officier brave, habile et expérimenté, *arriva des Indes Occidentales, où il*

M. Féret obtained this valuable document from a resident in Dieppe, where it has been for an unknown time; and it is more than probable that it had been in the possession of M. de Chastes, governor of the town and castle of Dieppe, who was Champlain's chief friend and protector, under whose auspices he had been employed in the war in Brittany against the League, and by whom, after his return from the West Indies, he was sent to Canada. To him, it is most likely that Champlain would present a narrative of his voyage. On M. de Chastes' death, the manuscript probably passed into the possession of the Convent of the Minimes at Dieppe, to which he was a great benefactor during his life, and by testament after his death. He was also, by his desire, buried in the church of the convent. The library of the Minime fathers was, with the rest of their property, and that of the other convents of the town, dispersed at the great Revolution; but most of the books remained at Dieppe, as may be seen by a reference to the numerous works which have gradually found their way, by gift or purchase, to the " Public Library" of that town,

avoit passé deux ans et demi. Le Commandeur de Chatte lui proposa de faire le voyage de Canada, et il y consentit avec l'agrément du Roy, etc."—Ed.

bearing inscriptions as having belonged to the convent.

The readers of Champlain's *Voyages in New France*, will remember the allusion to the expedition which is the subject of the following narrative: " Sur ces entrefaites," he says, speaking of the projects of Monsieur de Chastes for the Canadian voyage, " je me trouvais en cour, venu fraischement des Indes Occidentales, où j'avois été près de deux ans et demy après que les Espagnols furent partis de Blavet, et la paix foict en France, où pendant les guerres j'avais servi sa dicte majesté (Henry IV) souz Messeigneurs le Mareschal d'Aumont de St. Luc, et le Mareschal de Brissac."

The relation of this voyage was never published, and this should rather confirm the supposition that the manuscript had been presented to M. Chastes. It was evidently finished in haste; as the omission of several drawings, which are mentioned but not inserted, and the character of the writing, shews. Champlain returned from this voyage early in 1602, and before the autumn of the year was occupied in making preparations for his first voyage to Canada, before his return from which in the next year, 1603, M. de Chastes had died. Had Champlain kept the manuscript of his West India voyage, he would

surely have published it in 1604, at the same time
that the account of his first expedition to Canada
was printed, and to none is it so likely that he would
have given his " Brief Discourse" as to his best friend
and patron, at whose death (he died at Dieppe) it
would pass into private hands, or the Minime Convent, and be lost sight of.

The narrative is highly interesting as exhibiting
the state of some of the West India Islands two
hundred and fifty years ago, many of them being
then uninhabited by Europeans; and of the condition of Mexico, and of the Spanish policy there,
where no foreigner was then permitted to set his
foot. Gage, who travelled some five and twenty
years after Champlain, bears witness to the difficulty
of proceeding thither, being obliged to hide himself
in an empty biscuit-cask to avoid the search of the
Spanish officials, till the vessel in which he had embarked should sail.

The account of the capture of Porto-rico, by the
Earl of Cumberland, and the state in which it appeared, after the English had abandoned the island,
is curious; and the combat with the Anglo-Franco-
Flemish fleet, amusing. The idea of the junction of
the Pacific and Atlantic Oceans is also remarkable.

The accuracy of Champlain's observations of all

that he saw, is evident; as to the hearsay descriptions, we may entertain doubts of the fidelity of his informant, but not of the good faith of the narrator. He had a certain amount of credulity in his character, the more remarkable in a man of such natural penetration and sagacity; but the belief in strange monsters was prevalent before, during, and for a long time after, his epoch; and it was the more to be excused from the hermetically closed state of the Spanish colonies, and the strange stories to which the consequent mystery gave rise. The curious details of the " Brief Discourse" seemed worthy of the attention of the geographer, the naturalist, and of the inquiring general reader. As the founder of the capital of our principal North American colony, Champlain's name is, in some sort, associated with English adventure. With that idea, permission was requested of M. Féret, to translate this narrative into English, which was most kindly and unhesitatingly granted by him. In the translation, endeavour has been made to preserve Champlain's style, as much as possible. The drawings are fac-similes of those in the manuscript. Discoverers are general benefactors: after a time, all nations profit by their labours. In Champlain's case, we are the principal gainers; but for his indomitable courage, enterprise, and determination, Quebec might never have existed, the colonization of Canada have been indefinitely retarded, and instead of a valuable country, advanced in civilization, and sufficing to itself, England might have conquered only a small colony struggling for existence, or scattered and insignificant settlements, feebly subsisting on a precarious and badly organized trade with native tribes. For nearly a century Champlain's predecessors had endeavoured, with all means and appliances, to found colonies in various parts of North America; all failed, and, for long after his time, Canada remained in a semi-torpid state. It required the solid foundations laid down by Champlain, to enable the young settlement to pass through the struggles of its infancy and arrive at maturity. None were found capable of carrying out his views for years after his death. Had he died earlier, no one could have replaced him; had he not lived, in all probability expedition after expedition would, as before, have been sent out with the same success which had attended all previous attempts, from Cartier to De la Roche.

Notes have been made on the various subjects which appear to require some explanation.

BIOGRAPHICAL NOTICE OF CHAMPLAIN.

It will be well, perhaps, to preface the notice of Champlain's career with a rapid sketch of the various expeditions, discoveries, and attempts at colonisation, of the French in North America, from the discoveries of Sebastian Cabot, in 1497, to the beginning of the seventeenth century.

The errors, disasters, and failures of his predecessors will throw out in stronger relief the sound common sense and sagacity, the determined courage and unfaltering resolution, and the prudent wariness, which enabled Champlain to note and avoid their errors, to meet and to overcome difficulties, to foresee and to prepare for possible evil contingencies.

It is certain that the French were among the first, if not the very first, who followed in the track, and profited by the discovery, of Cabot. The Basques, Bretons, and Normans, as early as 1504, practised the cod fishery along the coast and on the Great Bank of Newfoundland[1]—the ancestors, probably, of

---

[1] The Père Fournier, in his *Hydrographie*, says that the Basques and Bretons had been there before 1504 : " L'an 1504, ainsi qu'il

the Basques and Bretons who, a century later, so
stoutly resisted the pretensions of the companies
which were then forming, to the exclusive privilege
of the fishery and trade in those parts.

In 1506, Jean Denys, of Harfleur, published a
map of the newly known country, and, two years
after, a pilot of Dieppe, named Thomas Aubert,
commanding a vessel named the " Pensée," belonging
to Jean Ange, father of the celebrated Vicomte de
Dieppe, brought a North American Indian with him
to France.[1]

In the year 1518, the Baron de Léry undertook a
voyage to North America with the intention of forming a settlement; but, being detained at sea for a
long time, was obliged to return to France without

est porté dans l'histoire de Niflet, et dans Magin, les Basques,
Normands, et Bretons allèrent en la coste des Moreïes, dit le Grand
banc, vers le Cap Breton; voire, il semble qu'ils y ayent esté bien
auparavant, car dans une lettre écrite par Sebastian Cavot à
Henry VII, Roy d'Angleterre, l'an 1497, ces terres sont appelées du
nom d'Isles de Bacaleos, comme d'un nom assez connu. On ne
peut douter que ce nom ne leur ait este donné par les Basques, qui
seuls en Europe appellent ce poisson Bacaleos, ou Bacallos : et les
originaires l'appellent Apagé."—Lib. vi, c. 12, Paris, 1643. Others
say that Juan Vaz de Cortereal explored the northern seas and discovered the land of *Baccalhos*, or Codfishland, in 1463, either of
which, if true, accounts for Cabot's mentioning the name as fami-
liar, but overthrows his claim to its discovery... Champlain also
writes : " Ce furent les Bretons et les Normands qui en l'an 1504
descouvrirent, *les premiers des Chréstiens*, le Grand Banc des
Moluques (Molues or Morues) et les Isles de Terre Neufve, ainsi
qu'il se remarque és histoires de Niflet et d'Antoine Maginus."—
Voyages de la Nouvelle France, Paris, 1632.

[1] Navarrete and Ramusio.

accomplishing his object, leaving on the Isle des Sables (Sable Island) and at Campseau (Canso) his cattle and pigs, which multiplied considerably, and were subsequently of the greatest service to certain of the Marquis de la Roche's people, who, about eighty years later, were left on Sable Island, without any other resource but fish and the flesh of the cattle they found there.[1]

In 1524, Francis I sent Giovanni Ferazzano, a Florentine, on an expedition of discovery to the coast of North America. The only document extant of this (first) voyage is a letter from Ferazzano to the king, dated the 8th July, 1524,[2] wherein he supposes that His Majesty is acquainted with his progress, the events of the voyage, and the success of this first attempt. In the following year he again sailed, and in March arrived at the coast of Florida. He ranged the coast from about the 30th to the 50th degree north latitude, as far as an island which the Bretons had before discovered.[3] Ferazzano took possession, in the name of the most Christian king, of all the country which he visited. The next year he undertook a third voyage, of which nothing authentic was ever known, save that he perished in it.[4]

[1] Fournier.

[2] Ramusio. Mark Lescarbot, who wrote a history of New France (Paris, 1612), also gives a detailed account of the voyages of Ferazzano.

[3] Bruzen de la Martonière, *Dictionnaire Geographique*, Paris, 1768.

[4] Fournier quaintly says : "Il avait l'intention d'aller jusques au Pôle, mais il fust pris et mangé par des sauvages."

In 1534, Jacques Cartier, of St. Malo,[1] sailed thence on the 20th April, with two vessels of the burthen of sixty tons each, furnished by Philippe Chabot, admiral of France, and the Comte de Brion, for the purpose of continuing the discoveries of Ferazzano, and on the 10th May arrived at Cape Bonavista, in Newfoundland. After some discoveries in that island he proceeded to the southward, and entering the great gulf, explored a bay, which he named La Baye des Chaleurs. The rigour of the season prevented his pursuing his discoveries that year, and he returned to France.

At the instance of Charles de Moïry, sieur de la Maillères, then vice-admiral of France, Cartier returned in the following year to the gulf, to which he gave the name of Saint Lawrence, subsequently extended to the great river which flows into it, and which the natives called the river of Canada. On the 15th August, he discovered the island of Naliscolet, calling it Isle de l'Assomption, now Anticosti. On the 1st September he arrived at the Saguenay river, flowing into the St. Lawrence. He ascended the latter stream to an island about a hundred and twenty leagues from the sea, which he named Isle d'Orléans, and wintered at a little river which he called Ste. Croix, afterwards rivière St. Charles. He then continued his voyage up the St. Lawrence to a place called Hochelaga, a large Indian village on an island at the foot of a mountain which

---

[1] Champlain says that he was "fort étendu et experimenté au faict de la marine, autant qu'autre de son temps."

he called Mont Royal, and which, altered to Montréal, is now the name of the whole island. Finding it impossible (according to his report) to surmount the rapids (Sault St. Louis), he returned to his vessels, but was obliged again to winter on the banks of a small river falling into the Ste. Croix, and which he named "the river Jacques Cartier." The greater part of his people died of scurvy, and Cartier, discontented and disappointed at the little progress he had made, and grieved for the loss of his people, returned to France. " And thinking the air was so contrary to our nature that we could hardly live there, having so suffered during the winter from the disease of the scurvy, which he called ' mal de terre,' he so made his relation to the king and the vice-admiral de Maillères, who not looking deeply into the matter, the enterprise was fruitless. And, to say truth, those who have the conduct of discoveries are often the cause of the failure of the best plans, if their reports are too implicitly trusted ; for in thus entirely confiding in them, enterprises are judged to be impossible, or so traversed by difficulties, that they cannot be carried out, save with almost insupportable expenses and pains."[1]

In 1541, Jean François de la Roque, sieur de Roberval, a gentleman of Picardy, was named viceroy of Nouvelle France, and renewed the attempt to form a colony in Canada. He first sent out Cartier as his deputy, to commence a settlement in the island of Mont Royal, and despatched one of his pilots,

---

[1] Champlain, *Voyages en Nouvelle France*, etc.

Jean Alphonse, of Saintonge, one of the best French navigators of his time, to reconnoitre the coast beyond Labrador, and to endeavour to find a shorter passage for Eastern commerce than round Cape Horn or the Straits of Magellan ; but, meeting with great obstacles and risk from the ice, Alphonse was obliged to return. The proposed settlement had no better success. Cartier remained nearly eighteen months abandoned to his own resources, as De Roberval, who was to have shortly followed him, delayed his departure, and when at last he set out on his voyage, he met Cartier on his way back to France, having lost many of his people, and suffered extreme distress from famine. De Roberval wished to force him to return to Canada, but Cartier refused.

The next expedition was that of Jean Ribaut, of Dieppe, a Protestant, and one of the best sea captains in France. He was despatched under the auspices of the Admiral de Coligny to establish a colony in that part of Florida visited by Ferazzano in his second voyage. Ribaut set sail on the 18th February, 1562, and landed at a cape which he named Cape François. Pursuing his course towards the north, he disembarked at the " Rivière de Mai," setting up a stone pillar with the arms of France affixed, in token of taking possession of the country. Continuing about sixty leagues more to the northward, he built a fort, which he styled Charles fort, on about the spot where Charleston was subsequently founded by the English. The fort finished, Ribaut found that his provisions were running short, and that he could not

that year make the purposed settlement. He therefore left eighteen men in the fort, under the command
of a Captain Albert, with all the supplies that he
could spare, and set sail for France in July, promising
to return to revictual his people and establish the
colony. Unfortunately, on his arrival in France he
was employed in the war which had just broken out
with Spain, and could not accomplish his promise.

Captain Albert and his men, trusting to Ribaut's
coming back with ample stores, did not trouble themselves to clear and cultivate land, so as to be prepared
in case of delay or accident, but consumed their provisions without order or care, so that in a short time
they were reduced to great scarcity. The men
mutinied, hung one of their comrades for some trifling
cause, and becoming more violent from want and
impunity, killed their commander Albert, electing in
his place one Nicolas Barré, " a good sort of a man !"
No succour arriving, they built a small vessel to endeavour to return to France, and put to sea with the
scanty remains of their stock of provisions. In a
very few days that was exhausted, and the famine
became so terrible and reduced them to such extremity that they were obliged to cast lots which of
them should be killed to support the others. " And,"
says Fournier, " what is greatly to be admired, the
lot fell on the man who had been the cause of the
mutiny against Captain Albert." Fortunately, the
survivors were picked up by an English ship and
carried to England.

In 1564 René de Laudonnière was sent to Florida

by Admiral de Coligny. He sailed on the 22nd of
April, and duly arrived at the Rivière de Mai, where
he built a fort, which he named La Caroline, re-
christened by the Spaniards " San Matteo." As in
the case of Captain Albert, a conspiracy was formed
against Laudonnière, his men mutinied, and threatened to kill him if he would not allow them to go to
sea and pillage the Virgin Islands and the coast of St.
Domingo : Laudonnière was forced to consent. The
mutineers fitted out a small vessel, captured and
plundered some Spanish ships, but after cruising for
some time were obliged to return to La Caroline,
where Laudonnière, resuming his authority, had four
of them hanged. In addition to these troubles, before
the winter was past, their provisions began to fail,
and after subsisting for more than six weeks on
roots, and no supplies arriving from France, they
determined to build a vessel, so as to be able to return
there in August ; but the famine becoming more
and more severe, the men were too weak to finish
their barque. Many went among the Indians, who
mocked and ill treated them, upon which they
attacked the savages and obtained some maize, which
strengthened and gave them courage to work at their
vessel. They then prepared to demolish the fort
before setting sail for Europe ; but while thus occupied, four ships were seen off the coast, which
proved to be English, who, on seeing the extremity
to which the French were reduced, assisted them
with provisions, and helped them to complete their
vessel. When ready to embark, Laudonnière again

descried some ships approaching the coast; this time they were French, commanded by Ribaut, who was bringing succour and the means of increasing the settlement.

Ribaut had been again despatched by the Admiral de Coligny with six ships and about six hundred men, chiefly Protestants, to complete the establishment of the long-desired colony. He set sail from Dieppe in June, 1565, and arrived at his destination on the 25th August. The Spaniards had doubtless been informed of this expedition, as before Ribaut could disembark his men and stores, a squadron of large ships was seen in the offing. He sent his son to reconnoitre, following shortly with his other vessels. A violent tempest arose, his ships were driven on shore, and many of his men drowned. With the remainder he retired to his little fort, almost without arms or ammunition. The Spaniards (although then at peace with France) stormed it, and massacred all in it, men, women, and children. Ribaut, although promised his life, was at last stabbed in cold blood by a Spanish captain, named Vallemande, and his body treated with atrocious barbarity,--his head and face were flayed; the skin, with the hair and beard attached, dried, and sent to the nearest Spanish colony. The Spaniards then hung the bodies of the slain, and all the French whom they could catch, on the nearest trees, with an inscription to the effect that " these men are not hung as Frenchmen, but as heretics."

Laudonnière with a few men escaped into the

woods, and returned after some time to France. The son of Ribaut also, escaping both the storm and the Spanish squadron, arrived there in safety. The king of France made some remonstrances about this horrible affair to his brother sovereign, the king of Spain, who disavowed the deed, but gave no redress.

Ribaut was, however, well avenged by one of his own creed. In 1567, Dominique de Gourgues, a Calvinist gentleman of Gascony, fitted out two (some say three) ships, at his own cost, and proceeded to Florida. Assisted by the natives, with whom he formed an alliance, he attacked and took by assault the Spanish forts, treating the Spaniards as they had treated the French, by hanging them all on the same trees, altering the inscription to the purport that " these men are not hung as Spaniards, but as traitors, robbers, and murderers." He then demolished the forts, and returned to France in 1568, performing the voyage, it is said, in seventeen days.

The king of Spain in his turn complained, and De Gourgues, disavowed and threatened with condign punishment by his sovereign, was obliged to absent himself. He seems, however, to have kept his ire warm against the Spaniards, as in 1582 we find him in the service of Don Antonio, of Portugal, who named him admiral of the fleet which he was equipping against Spain ; but, on the point of sailing, De Gourgues was seized with a mortal malady, and died,—thus disappointing the hopes of his old enemy the king of Spain, who had offered a large sum for his head.

In the year 1591, a voyage to Canada was undertaken by the sieur du Court Pré Ravillon, in a vessel called the Bonaventure, to endeavour to establish a trade in moose-skins and teeth. Whether he succeeded in his adventure or not, history is silent.

The Marquis de la Roche fitted out some vessels in 1591, embarking a number of men and a large quantity of stores of all kinds requisite for forming a colony in Canada. Not having, it appears, any personal knowledge of the country or of navigation, he engaged a Norman pilot, of the name of Chédotel, for the voyage. The details of this enterprise are not very clear, but it is certain that the expedition reached the Isle des Sables, and, for some reason or other, seventeen of the people were sent on shore and abandoned. The poor fellows remained there for seven years, living in holes in the ground, and subsisting on fish and the cattle which they found wild in considerable numbers—the descendants of those left there in 1518 by the Baron de Léry.[1]

At the expiration of seven years, the pilot Chédotel was *condemned* by the Parliament of Rouen to go and fetch away the unfortunate men,—with the condition, however, that he was to have half of all the property, hides, oil, seal and black fox skins, etc., which the wretched creatures might have collected during their banishment.

On their arrival in France, the poor men were presented to the king, Henry IV, who ordered the

---

[1] Champlain says, that the cattle had been saved from the wreck of a Spanish ship.

Duke de Sully to give them some relief,—which the worthy Duke did, to the amount of fifty crowns each, "to encourage them to return there!"

The poor Marquis de la Roche, unfortunate in his expedition, was equally so at court in his endeavours to obtain the aid which the king had promised him. "It being denied him," says Champlain, "at the instigation of certain persons who had no wish that the true worship of God should increase, or to see the Catholic, Apostolic, and Roman religion flourish in those parts."

The Marquis took all this so much to heart that he fell sick and died, having consumed all his property, and wasted his time and labour, in vain.

In the year following (1599), the sieur Chauvin, de Ponthuict, captain in the Royal Marine, at the persuasion of Captain du Pont Gravé of St. Malo, (both Protestants), obtained a privilege for ten years, at the charge of forming a company for the colonization of Canada. Having equipped his vessels, he gave the command of one of them to Du Pont Gravé, and proceeding to the river St. Lawrence, arrived in safety at Tadoussac, at the junction of the Saguenay with that river. One of the objects which they were bound mainly to follow was the propagation of the Roman Catholic religion among the savages. Chauvin's people were for the most part Catholics, but the chiefs were Calvinists, which was not precisely adapted for the fulfilment of the projected purpose, " but that," again says Champlain, " was what they thought of the least."

Chauvin resolved to remain at Tadoussac, in spite of the remonstrances of Du Pont Gravé, who wished him to proceed higher up the river, having already been to "Three Rivers" in a previous voyage, trading with the Indians. M. de Monts (of whom we shall hear more hereafter), who had made the voyage with them for his pleasure, agreed with Du Pont Gravé, but Chauvin was obstinate, and set about erecting a habitation in the most disagreeable and unproductive spot in the country,—full of rocks, fir and birch trees, the land unfit for cultivation, and the cold so excessive, that " if there be an ounce of cold forty leagues up the river, there is a pound at Tadoussac."[1]

Chauvin posted sixteen men at a little stream near the house, to which they might retire upon occasion. The stores (little enough) were at the mercy of all, and soon began to run short, whereupon Chauvin returned to France, taking Du Pont Gravé and De Monts with him.

The men remaining at the intended settlement, quickly consumed the little provision left, and " the winter coming on soon taught them the difference between France and Tadoussac,—it was the court of king Petault, where every man commanded."[2] Indolence and carelessness, with sickness, soon did their work, and they were reduced to the necessity of giving themselves up to the Indian tribes around, who received them kindly. Many died, and all suffered extremely.

Chauvin, in 1600, prepared another expedition,

---

[1] Champlain.   [2] Ibid., *Voyages en Nouvelle France*, etc.

which from the same causes was as fruitless as the first. He fitted out a third on a larger scale, but was not able to carry out his new plans, being attacked by a malady " which sent him to the other world."[1]

We have now arrived at the period of Champlain's first connection with Canadian discovery and colonization. The difficulties, dangers—not to say horrors —of the previous expeditions were enough to deter any but the most confident and resolute from attempting such an apparently hopeless task; but the hour and the man were come, and from the date of Chauvin's death a new era was to arise for Canada, and French colonization in North America was at last—to be.

Samuel Champlain, descended from a noble family of Saintonge, was born at Brouage,[2] a place formerly of some importance in that province, now an obscure town of the department of the Charente Inférieure. Of the date of his birth and of his earlier career there is no account extant; from the events of the last thirty-five or thirty-six years of his life we may, however, form a correct judgment of his attainments, which, in navigation, in military matters, and in

---

[1] Desmarquets, in his *Mémoires Chronologiques pour servir à l'Histoire de la Ville de Dieppe*, says that Chauvin, on arriving at Tadoussac the second time, found only the corpses of the sixteen men whom he had left there. When he again returned to France he left twenty more men, but death preventing his intended third voyage, those twenty died of hunger, like the sixteen first.

[2] The salt works at Brouage were considered the finest in the kingdom. Cardinal Richelieu also established a large cannon foundry there in 1627.

general knowledge, were evidently of no common order. That he had early distinguished himself is also clear, and that his services were appreciated we may gather from the high favour with which he was regarded by the king, and from the friendship and constant protection with which he was honoured by one of the best and bravest, as well as most intelligent and devoted followers of Henry IV,—the Sieur Aymar de Chastes, governor of the town and château of Dieppe, who commanded the fleet appointed to cruize on the coast of Brittany during the latter years of the war with the League and the Spaniards,[1] and under whose orders Champlain had served. On Champlain's return from the voyage to the West Indies, of which the narrative is now for the first time published, he learned that Chauvin was dead, and that his friend, Mons. de Chastes, undeterred by the previous failures and disasters, had resolved to undertake the establishment of a colony in Canada,

---

[1] The Commander Aymar de Chastes, also styled Frère Aymar de Clermont, was knight and maréschal of the order of St. John of Jerusalem, of the language of Auvergne, commander of the Armeteau and of St. Paul, lieutenant-general for the king in the Pays de Coer, and governor of the town and castle of Dieppe. He was employed by Henry III to reinstate Don Antonio of Portugal in his kingdom, and by Henry IV to command the fleet on the coast of Brittany; it was almost entirely owing to Mons. de Chastes that Dieppe declared for the king against the League, which enabled him to fight and win the battle of Arques. He died at Dieppe, on the 13th of May, 1603, and was buried in the church of the Minimes there, followed to the grave by all the inhabitants, "who looked on him as their father and protector," says Asselini, MS. Chron.

and even to proceed thither and devote the remainder of his well-spent life to the prosecution of the enterprise. The cause and manner of Champlain's embarking in the undertaking cannot be better narrated than in his own words.

" The fourth enterprise was that of the Sieur Commander de Chastes, a very honourable man, a good catholic, and worthy servant of the king, whom he had faithfully served on many signal occasions, and although his head was charged with grey hairs as with years, he resolved to proceed thither in person, and dedicate the remainder of his life to the service of his God and of his king, by fixing his residence and living and dying there gloriously : so he hoped, if God had not withdrawn him from this world sooner than he thought. He had very Christian designs, to which I can bear good witness, he having done me the honour of communicating somewhat of them. Soon after the death of Chauvin he obtained a new commission from the king, and as the expenses were very great, he formed a company with several gentlemen and with the principal merchants of Rouen and other places, on certain conditions : this being done, vessels were prepared, as well for the execution of the main design, as for discovery and peopling the country. Du Pont Gravé, as one who had already made the voyage and noticed the faults of the past, was (with commission from his majesty) chosen to proceed to Tadaussac, thence to go and examine the Sault St. Louis and the country beyond, in order to make a report on his return for the better prepara-

tion of a second voyage, when the said commander,
De Chastes, would quit his government (of Dieppe),
and, with the permission of his majesty, who truly
loved him, proceed to the country of New France.

" While this was going on, I found myself at court,
being freshly returned from the West Indies, where
I had been nearly two years and a half, after the
Spaniards had quitted Blavet, where, during the wars,
I had served His Majesty under Messeigneurs the
Maréchal d'Aumont de St. Luc and the Maréchal de
Brissac."

" Going from time to time to see the said sieur de
Chastes, judging that I might serve him in his design,
he did me the honour, as I have said, to communicate
something of it to me, and asked me if it would be
agreeable to me to make the voyage to examine the
country, and see what those engaged in the undertaking should do. I told him that I was very much
his servant, but that I could not give myself license
to undertake the voyage without the commands of
the king, to whom I was bound, as well by birth as by
the pension with which His Majesty honoured me
to enable me to maintain myself near his person,[1] but
that, if it should please him to speak to the king
about it, and give me his commands, that it would
be very agreeable to me, which he promised and did,

[1] This fact at once shews that Champlain's fortune was but
small and his merits great. Henry IV at that time had no funds
to throw away, and a pension then given must have been well
deserved. The attachment to his person also proves the feeling
of the king.

d

and received the king's orders for me to make the voyage and make a faithful report thereof; and for that purpose M. de Gesvres, secretary of his Commandments, sent me with a letter to the said Du Pont Gravé, desiring him to take me in his ship, and enable me to see and examine what could be done in the country, giving me every possible assistance."

" Me voilà expédié," continues Champlain, who immediately left Paris, and embarking with Du Pont Gravé, had a favourable voyage to Tadoussac, from whence they proceeded up the St. Lawrence in small vessels of twelve to fifteen tons burthen. At Sault St. Louis, Du Pont Gravé and Champlain, with five men, continued with great difficulty about a league further, to the foot of the rapids; where, finding it impossible to proceed with their skiff, on account of the rocks and rushing waters, all they could do was to land and examine the course and difficulties of the rapids, explore the surrounding country, and obtain accounts from the Indians as to the inhabitants, the productions, and the sources of the principal rivers, particularly of the St. Lawrence.

Champlain prepared a *petit discours*, or report, with an exact chart of all that had been seen and explored, and they then returned to Tadoussac, having made but little progress; rejoining their people, who had been employed in the interim in trading with the natives, they set sail for France.

When Champlain arrived at Honfleur, he learned the death of his friend and patron, the commander De Chastes, " which greatly afflicted me, well know-

ing that it would be difficult for another to undertake the enterprise without being opposed, unless
it should be some nobleman, whose authority was
capable of overcoming envy."

From Honfleur he proceeded directly to Paris, to
present his " *discours fort particulier,*" and the Map
which he had made, to the king, who was much grati-
fied, and promised not to abandon the design, but
rather to pursue and favour it.

After the death of Monsieur de Chastes, the Sieur
de Monts,[1] who had already been to Canada with
Chauvin, desirous of following the example of Monsieur de Chastes, completed the arrangements with
the merchants of Rouen, Dieppe, La Rochelle, etc.,
which had been prepared by his predecessor, for the
formation of a company for colonization in New
France ; but not on the St. Lawrence, the specimen
he had seen of the country when with Chauvin having
taken away all desire to return there, particularly as
he wished to settle more to the southward, in a milder
and more agreeable climate.

De Monts, who was of the " pretended-reformed

---

[1] Pierre du Gast, sieur de Monts, gentleman of the chamber to
the king, was named in 1603 vice-admiral of the coasts of Acadia,
from the fortieth to the forty-sixth degree of north latitude, and in
the following year his majesty gave him the lieutenancy of the
same country. By letters patent of 21st January, 1605, all subjects, save De Monts and his associates, were forbidden to trade
in those parts. De Monts first named the sieur Du Pont Gravé
his lieutenant in September 1605, and in February 1606 replaced
him by the sieur de Paitrincourt. The cession to De Monts was
again ratified in 1608, but to little purpose.

religion," undertook to establish the Roman Catholic and Apostolic religion in his colony, but every one was to be free to live according to his creed.

All preliminaries being settled, De Monts fitted out three ships, with all things necessary, not only for trading in peltries at Tadoussac, but for establishing a settlement elsewhere; taking out a number of gentlemen, and all kinds of artisans, with soldiers and others of both religions, not forgetting priests and ministers.

Being ready to depart, De Monts proposed to Champlain to accompany him, and the desire to revisit and see more of the country having grown stronger within him, he readily promised to go, always with the king's permission, which was willingly granted; being ordered, moreover, by his Majesty to make to him a faithful report of all that he should see and discover.

They all embarked at Dieppe in 1603: one vessel proceeded to Tadoussac; another, commanded by Du Pont Gravé, went to Campseau (Canso) and along the coast towards the island of Cape Breton, to look after certain adventurers trading there in contravention of the king's prohibition. De Monts, with Champlain, took his course to the coast of Acadia, and the weather being very favourable, in a month arrived off Cape la Héve. De Monts continued along the coast, seeking some convenient spot for his settlement, sending Champlain also with a pilot to examine the coast for the same purpose. They discovered a number of ports and rivers, and De Monts at last fixed on an island which he thought well adapted to his purpose ; the situation strong, the land good, and the temperature mild. He therefore set about discharging his vessels and building shelter for his people, and when all that was done he sent back the ships with Mons. de Paitrincourt, who had replaced Du Pont Gravé as his lieutenant, and who had gone out to see the country with the intention of settling there.

During this time (fully three years) Champlain occupied himself in exploring the whole coast of Acadia (Nova Scotia), from Cape la Héve, in latitude 45° 5' ; examining all the bays, creeks, mouths of rivers, and islands of the great Baye Françoise (so named by him), now the Bay of Fundy, coasting on to " Cape Fortuné," in latitude 41° 20' (now Cape Cod), and a few leagues farther, to a headland, which, with a great shoal near it, he called " Mallebarre", from the dangers he had there experienced. To the northward he examined the land from Cape la Héve to Cape Canso and Cape Breton, and, his arduous labours terminated, he returned with De Monts to France in 1607.

On their arrival, they found that great complaints had been made by certain Bretons, Basques, and others, of the excesses committed by the captains of De Monts' vessels while on their cruise, and of the ill-treatment they had sustained from them and their crews, who had seized their property, detained their persons, and deprived them of all traffic that had hitherto been free to them ; so that, if the king did

not interfere and take some order about it, all that
navigation would be lost, the customs diminished,
themselves ruined, and their wives and children, poor
and miserable, obliged to beg their bread. It seems,
though, that the poor Bretons and their companions
were able to bribe pretty highly; as, in consequence
of this outcry, and the intrigues of some influential
persons at court, who promised to equip and keep
three hundred men in the country, the commission
or privilege of De Monts was revoked, " as the price
of a certain sum, which a certain person received,
without the king's knowing anything about it," says
Champlain.

Thus was De Monts rewarded for having expended
upwards of one hundred thousand livres, and passed
more than three years of great suffering, from long
duration of the snows and extreme cold, and having
lost more than half his people by the dreaded " mala-
die de terre", or earth sickness.

As compensation, however, for his losses, the Royal
Council generously granted him six thousand livres;
not in ready money, but to be paid by such vessels
as should traffic in peltry, etc., in the new country;
but De Monts was obliged to abandon even this
mockery of a grant, finding the expense of collecting
greater than the receipts. Champlain at this exclaims indignantly: " Thus were affairs managed in
the Council of his majesty; may God pardon those
whom He has called to Himself, and amend the
living! Hé! bon Dieu! who would ever undertake
anything, if all can be revoked in such a fashion,

without carefully examining affairs before deciding. Those also who know least cry out the loudest, and pretend to know more than men of tried experience." He adds that there was one great defect in De Monts' expedition—the mixture of creeds, " as two contrary religions never produce much fruit for the glory of God among the heathen they wish to convert." " I have seen," says he, " the minister and our curé fight with their fists about differences of religion, and," he continues slyly, " I do not know which was the bravest or hit the hardest blows, but I do very well know that the minister complained sometimes to Mons. de Monts of having been soundly beaten ; and in this way they cleared up the points of controversy. I leave you to think if it was very pleasant to behold. The savages were sometimes on one side, sometimes on the other ; and the French, divided according to their different belief, said everything that was bad, both of one and the other religion. These quarrels were really the means of rendering the infidel more hardened in his infidelity."

In the following year (1608) De Monts, desirous of making another attempt, consulted with Champlain, who advised him to proceed direct to the river St. Laurence, with which he was well acquainted from the experience of his previous voyage. De Monts, adopting his advice, applied again to the king, who granted him another commission authorising him to make the desired settlement ; and to enable him the better to bear the expenses, interdicted the trade in peltry to all others for one year.

Upon this De Monts fitted out two vessels at Honfleur, and named Champlain his deputy or lieutenant in New France. One of the ships was commanded by Du Pont Gravé, who sailed first for Tadoussac, and Champlain followed with all things necessary for the intended settlement, arriving happily at Tadoussac. He then landed his people and stores, and proceeded up the river to seek for a convenient spot for his purpose, and finding at the narrowest part of the stream a place called by the natives Quebec, which seemed suitable, he there resolved to establish his colony, and accordingly transported thither all his men and goods with as little delay as possible. He then immediately caused dwellings to be erected, gardens prepared and planted, and land cleared and sown.

It was on the 3rd of July, 1608, that Champlain first arrived at Quebec; the remainder of the season and the winter were fully occupied with the necessary works of lodging the people, apportioning and clearing land, getting supplies of firing, etc., and exploring the country in the more immediate neighbourhood. On the 18th of May in the next year, Champlain proceeded to examine the river above the new settlement. At the little island of St. Eloy, near the river St. Marie, he fell in with a body of two or three hundred Indians, " Algenquins and Ochotiquens," who were on their way to Quebec to beg his assistance (which they reminded him he had promised ten moons before to the son of their chief) against the Iroquois, with whom they were at deadly feud. Champlain promised his aid, and returned with them to the settlement, where they remained for five or six days feasting and rejoicing. From thence he wrote to Du Pont Gravé, who was at Tadoussac, begging him to join him as soon as possible; and so soon as he arrived Champlain again left Quebec with the Indians, and on the 1st of June arrived at Saint Croix with a boat furnished with all things necessary for the expedition. From thence he continued to the Iroquois river, but finding that he could not pass the first rapid with his boat, as the natives had assured him, he resolved to pursue the journey in the canoes of the Indians. The greater part of his men refused to follow him, but, resolved to fulfil his promise, and desirous of visiting a great lake and beautiful country in the enemy's territory, which had been described to him by his allies, he determined on proceeding, with only two of his men, who volunteered to accompany him.

On the 2nd of July, the expedition left the rapids and ascended the Iroquois river to the lake above mentioned, where they were met by some two hundred of the enemy; a battle ensued, in which Champlain, at one shot of his arquebuss loaded with four balls, killed two of their chiefs and wounded another, which equally astonished both his friends and the enemies, who seeing their chiefs fall, fled, abandoning the field of battle and their village to the victors, who, after making good cheer, singing, and dancing, set out on their return with some ten or twelve prisoners.

Champlain gave his name to the lake on whose borders the action was fought, which it still retains.

On the way back, his Indian allies began tormenting one of their prisoners with the usual refinements of cruelty; which considerably disgusted Champlain, whom they requested " to do as they did." He angrily refused, but offered to put the poor wretch out of misery by shooting him at once with his arquebuss. Seeing that he was irritated, they told him he might do so, "and," says he naïvely, " so I did, without his seeing anything."

They soon arrived at Quebec, where he gave them " bread and peas and paternosters," to ornament the skulls of their enemies, as rejoicing on their return. The next day Champlain went with them in their canoes to Tadoussac, in order to witness their ceremonies; and does not omit to mention how the women stripped themselves stark naked, and threw themselves into the water to meet the canoes, taking the enemies' heads to hang round their necks as precious ornaments. His Indian friends also made him a present of some of their weapons and one of the heads " to show to his king," which to please them he promised.

From this first battle Champlain seems to have imbibed a taste for fighting the Iroquois (though why he mixed in the quarrel at all he does not explain), as in 1610 he again started from Quebec, with a boat and some of his people for the mouth of the Iroquois river, to join about four hundred Algenquins and others in another attack on their mortal enemies.

They found the Iroquois intrenched in a " fort" or
stockade, and after a sharp fight, in which Champlain
was wounded by an arrow in the ear and neck, and
one of his men in the arms, they stormed the " fort,"
assisted by the men whom he had left in the boat,
but who, hearing the firing, thought it shame to
remain idle while their comrades were fighting. On
leaving the Algenquins, they insisted on his taking
one of their young men with him as hostage for a
young French lad whom he left with them, at his
own desire, to learn their language, etc.

While Champlain was thus busily occupied, Mons.
de Monts, who was then governor of Pons, in Saintonge, having remained at Paris to settle some private affairs, was again attacked and worried by the
complaints of his former opponents, " the Bretons,
Basques, and Normans," and, they again getting the
ear of persons in power, De Monts was for the second
time deprived of his privilege, and this time without any compensation. He wrote an account of the
whole business to Champlain, who immediately returned to France, and, after having informed De
Monts of his labours at Quebec, made a full report of
all to the king, who received both him and it with
much satisfaction.

De Monts endeavoured by every possible means
to obtain a third commission, but his enemies were
too powerful, and so managed matters that all his
attempts and labour were in vain. Nevertheless,
being extremely desirous of settling in the new country, he resolved, with or without commission, to

continue his establishment there, and explore the country inland on the upper part of the St. Laurence; and for the better execution of the project he again equipped two ships, in conjunction with a company formed under the auspices of Father Coton (confessor to Henry IV) and of Madame de Guercheville, and which had obtained certain privileges for the establishment of a Jesuit mission in New France.[1] The vessels being ready, Champlain and Du Pont Gravé embarked with labourers and artisans of all kinds, and arriving at Tadoussac and Quebec, found all things in good and flourishing condition.

In 1611, in the early spring, Champlain started from Quebec in order to meet the Indians with the young Frenchman, and give back the hostages left at the settlement; but not finding them, he continued to explore the country as far as Mont Royal, or Montreal. Shortly after the natives arrived, and after

---

[1] The Jesuits did not send a mission until the next year, 1611. Madame de Guercheville was the wife of M. de Liancour, "premier écuyer" to the king, and governor of Paris : she was one of the most ardent supporters of the Jesuits, as the following trait will shew: "When the expedition of M. de Biencour, son of M. de Poitrincourt, was preparing at Dieppe in 1611, the Jesuits sent two of their company, the fathers Biart and Rémond Massé, to join it, and proceed to establish a mission in Canada. On their arrival at Dieppe, the Sieurs du Querne and Jourdain, Protestants and members of the Company of New France, would not allow them to embark, treating them with disdain and contumely. At which Madame de Guercheville was so indignant that, aided by the influence of Father Coton, she managed to force the recusant Protestants to quit the company, with an indemnity of four thousand livres for their shares."—Asselini, MS. Chronicle, 1682.

exchanging presents, he took leave of them, trusting another lad to their care, with particular instructions as to the observations he was to make while with them.   He returned to Quebec in June, and finding matters proceeding regularly he sailed for France, arriving at La Rochelle on the 11th of August.

On the 5th of March of the next year (1612), Champlain again embarked at Honfleur for Quebec, arriving on the 7th of May, and finding all who had wintered there in health and prospering.   The winter had been so mild that the river had not been frozen, " the trees also began to reclothe themselves with leaves, and the fields to be enameled with flowers."

On the 23rd, he left Quebec for the Sault St. Louis with two canoes, having with him only four men, one of whom was a certain Nicolas Vignan, " the most impudent liar that had been seen for a long time," as will presently appear.   One of Champlain's cherished projects was to endeavour to penetrate to the Arctic Sea by means of some of the rivers tributary to the St. Lawrence, which, by the account of the natives, had their sources in great lakes, from which other streams flowed towards the north.

This man Vignan had formerly wintered with the natives, and had been sent on journeys of exploration by Champlain on various occasions.   He had returned to Paris, where, in the commencement of the present year (1612), he had assured Champlain that he had seen the Northern Sea ; that the Algenquin river issued from a lake, which by another river discharged itself into the said sea, and that in seventeen

days he might go to it from Sault St. Louis. He
added that he had seen the wreck of an English ship
which had been lost on the coast, and that eighty
men had escaped to land, where they had all been
killed by the savages. He had been shown their
heads, which had been skinned (scalped) according
to their custom; and the Indians wished to present them to Champlain, with a young English boy
whom they had preserved.

"This news," says Champlain, "rejoiced me greatly,
thinking I had found near me that which I had
sought far off; so I conjured him to tell me the truth,
that I might inform the king. If his relation was
false he would put a rope round his neck, while if
what he said was true he would assuredly be well
recompensed. He assured me of the truth of his
statement with more oaths than ever, and to play his
part better, he gave me an account of the country,
which, he said, he had made as well as he could."
All these details, the assurance of the man, and the
air of simplicity which Champlain thought he perceived in him, combined with a knowledge of the
voyage which the English had made to Labrador
near that time, where they had wintered about the
63° of latitude and 250° of longitude, and had actu-
ally lost some vessels, induced him to give credence
to the man's story, and make a report of it to the
Chancellor. He also presented him to the Maréchal
de Brissac and other high personages, who strongly
recommended Champlain to look after the matter in
person. Upon this advice he procured a passage for

Vignan, in a vessel belonging to a Sieur Georges of La Rochelle, who, asking him why he was going out, etc., was also told by Vignan that he was going to show the Northern Ocean, which he had seen, to Champlain, and made a formal declaration to that effect before a notary of the town.

On taking leave of his companions before quitting Quebec, as before mentioned, Champlain again told Vignan that if his tale was not exactly true he had better not attempt the journey, as he would incur much risk; when Vignan again declared, on peril of his life, that all that he had averred was true.

On Monday, 27th May, Champlain accordingly left the island of Ste. Hélène on the expedition to discover the Northern Ocean, with four French and one Indian. The route that he followed is not clearly indicated; it is presumed that he ascended the Chaudière river to a lake, where he landed on an island, which he named Isle Sainte Croix. On the 6th of June he left this island, in company with a number of the natives who had joined him. About ten leagues further they arrived at some rapids, where the Indians purposed to leave their canoes, when a great dispute arose between them and Vignan, who declared there was no danger in passing them. The Indians told him he must be tired of life, and advised Champlain not to believe him, " for he spoke not the truth." Champlain followed the advice of the natives, and well it was for him, as Vignan sought all kinds of difficulties, either to get rid of, or to disgust him with the enterprise, as he afterwards confessed. Continuing his journey he fell in with a tribe of Indians, who wondered much how he had surmounted the dangers and difficulties of the rapids and the route, " saying he and his people must have fallen from the clouds," and wishing to know what his object was. Champlain told him that he had come to help them in their wars, and for that purpose he wished to proceed further on to visit and arrange with some other chiefs, which rejoiced them greatly ; so that they gave him two canoes to carry him on to the village of a great chief named " Tessouat," about eight leagues distant. This chief received him very well, though much astonished to see him, saying " he thought it was a dream, and could not believe what he beheld!"

On the following day a great council was held in the wigwam of Tessouat, with a preliminary feast, which gave Champlain occasion to protest against the Indian "cuisine," "because they cooked so dirtily." He asked them for fish and flesh, that he might prepare his dinner after his own fashion, "and for drink," says he, " we had fine clear water."

After much smoking and talking about his intentions of helping them to make war on their enemies, the Indians promised him four canoes, which gave him great joy ; " forgetting all my past troubles in the hope of beholding that much desired sea"; but he had rejoiced rather too soon, as his interpreter shortly after hastened to tell him that the Indians had again consulted together, and had come to the conclusion that if he undertook the desired journey,

then both he and they would die, so would not give
the four canoes; but that if he would defer the expedition to the next year, they would go with him.

Champlain, very much grieved at this change,
sought the chiefs, and told them boldly, that he
" had hitherto considered them as men, and truthful,
but that now they showed themselves to be children,
and lying !" and that if four canoes were too many,
to give two, and four of their people only.   The Indians again represented the difficulties of the way, of
the rapids, and the hostility of the people on the
route, and said that it was for fear of losing him that
they refused : to which he replied, that he had a man
with him, " showing them my impostor," who had
already been through the country, and had met with
neither the difficulties nor hostility that they mentioned.   It seems that Vignan had wintered with
this very Tessouat and his tribe, so that he had fallen
into a trap ; and the old chief turning to him, said,
" Nicolas, is it true that you have said that you had
been to the Nibericini ?"   Vignan was a long time
before answering, but at length said, " Yes, I have
been ;" on which the Indians rushed at him with
loud outcries, " as if they would eat him up or tear
him to pieces ; and Tessouat exclaimed, that he was
an impudent liar, well knowing that every night he
had slept at his side with his (Tessouat's) children,
and rose every morning with him, so that if he had
been with those people, it must have been during his
sleep.   " Let him be made to name the chiefs whom
he had seen, and describe the rivers, the rapids, the

f

lakes, and the country that he had passed," said the chief. Still Vignan affirmed anew, with many oaths, the truth of all that he had before said, and swore that he would proceed if the savages would give the canoes.

After some anxious private consideration of the probabilities and doubts, Champlain again called Vignan, and told him that the time was passed for dissimulation, and that now he must speak the truth, and he would forget the past; but that if he went further and found the statement false, he would assuredly have him hung or strangled; whereupon Vignan threw himself on his knees, and confessed that all that he had said in France and since was false; that he had never seen the Northern Sea, or been beyond the village of Tessouat, and had invented the whole story in order to return to Canada. Champlain, enraged, ordered him never to appear before him again, and immediately informed the Indians of the imposture; they proposed that Vignan should be left to them, and they would take care that he should tell no more lies, which Champlain declined. Finding his hopes thus frustrated and his journey at an end, on the 10th of June he took leave of Tessouat, and set out on his return, during which he met with nothing remarkable, save a false alarm of an attack of the enemy, and witnessing the offerings of the savages to the spirit of the Chaudière rapid. He arrived at the Sault St. Louis on the 17th, accompanied by certain of his Indian friends, with whom he made an agreement that they should

not trade without his permission. He made Vignan
again confess his lies in presence of his countrymen;
and, on his promising that he would retrieve his fault
by making a journey to the Northern Ocean and bring
back news of it in the following year, Champlain
pardoned him. He then proceeded to Tadoussac,
and, having nothing further to do that year in the
country, sailed for France on the 8th of August,
and in due time arrived at St. Malo.

I have dwelt somewhat at length on this episode
of Vignan's imposture, as it preeminently shows the
enterprising, persevering, and resolute character of
Champlain, combined with a generous and forgiving
disposition. Few at that time would have blamed
him for inflicting summary justice on the liar who
had so deceived him, or have condemned him had he
left Vignan to the tender mercies of Tessouat and
his tribe. The condition of pardon is also characteristic,—condemnation to perform the journey pretended to have been made, thus turning the imposture
to some advantage.

On his arrival in France, Champlain found the
affairs of the new company in great disorder, from
the detention of its chief protector, Monseigneur le
Prince de Condé, who had been created Viceroy of
Canada, " and this," says he, " made me judge that
the envious would not delay to vomit their poison,
and that they would now do that which before they
dared not; for the head being sick, the members cannot be healthy." After strange and scandalous intrigues which led to lawsuits, and consequently to

greater confusion, the associates of the company began to perceive that, with all these cabals, the colony
would be ruined and the company broken up, unless
they sent aid in men and materials to continue the
buildings and clearance of land.

Monsieur de Monts, always desirous to forward
the interests of his favorite settlement, drew up articles by which the company should be obliged to
furnish men, warlike stores, and provisions sufficient
for two years, while the new lands were being cleared
and cultivated; these articles were approved and laid
before the Royal Council. "But," says Champlain,
" I know not by what chance, all went off in smoke,
and God did not permit the said articles to be
accomplished."

During this time (in 1615) Champlain was at Honfleur, preparing for another voyage, when a certain
Boyer, one of the company, " as malicious as he was
litigious," attempted by chicane to deprive him of
the post of lieutenant for Monsieur le Prince, which
had been granted to him by letters patent, dated
15th October, 1612. "But all that did not touch
me ; having served as I had done, they could neither
take away my charge, nor the appointments to which
they had voluntarily obliged themselves when I had
arranged their association." This attempt to deprive
him of his well-earned honours, seems to have served
as a lesson to Champlain not to engage himself in
any way in the service of, or take share in, any of
the companies which were purely formed for prose-
cuting the colonization and trade of New France,

until the monopoly of the whole intercourse was
centred in a society, formed subsequently in 1627,
under the auspices and especial favour of the *de facto*
sovereign of France, Cardinal Richelieu. As lieutenant of the viceroys, he maintained a neutral position,
powerful enough to control hostility, without sub-
jecting himself to the influence of the cabals which
perpetually divided the parties, Jesuits, Recollets,
merchants, etc., who struggled for the chief power in
the various associations.

On the 24th of April, 1615, Champlain left Honfleur with four missionaries (Jesuits) on board his
vessel, and arrived without accident at Tadoussac on
the 25th May. He proceeded immediately to the
Sault St. Louis, when his first care was to arrange a
treaty with the friendly Indians to assist them in
their wars, on condition of their facilitating his enterprises of discovery, and with the view of advancing
the progress of Christianity among them. By helping
them to slay their enemies, he hoped to induce them
to worship his God !

The Indians were to furnish two thousand five
hundred warriors; and Champlain was to take as
many men as he could, and besides, to give his allies
some instruction in discipline, etc., which they received with great satisfaction, but, as by and by will
be seen, by which they profited little.

Having arranged this matter, Champlain returned
to the settlement to provide for the good conduct of
all affairs during his proposed absence, and, on the
9th of June, started with an interpreter and another

European, " myself third," he says, and ten savages, and by the Rivière des Prairies pursued his route to the Algenquin country ; from thence he continued by land to the lake of the Nipiserini (Lake Nipissing) in $45\frac{1}{4}°$ of latitude, where he arrived on the 26th of the same month, and remained two days; from thence he descended a river (Rivière des François) to the great Lake Attigouantan (Lake Huron), where he met some three hundred natives, with whom he " contracted friendship," making the chief a present of a hatchet, " with which he was as contented and joyful as if I had given him some rich present." The next day he continued his route along the shores of the lake to a village called Cahiagué, where the " army" was to rendezvous, having overtaken on the way thirteen or fourteen Frenchmen who had started before him from the Rivière des Prairies. He arrived at Cahiagué on the 17th of August, and was received with great gratitude and rejoicing by the Indians, who informed him that another and very warlike nation, the Entouhoronins (?), would join them with five hundred fighting men against the common enemy, —the Iroquois. The greater part of the " army" being assembled, they started together from the village on the 1st of September, and pursued their route, hunting as they went. On the 9th of October their scouts took eleven prisoners, " four women, one girl, three boys, and three men ;" whereupon one of the chiefs began tormenting a female prisoner by cutting off one of her fingers; at which Champlain indignantly interfered, and blamed the chief, " Cap-

tain Yroquet," severely, representing that it was unworthy of a warrior, as he called himself, to behave
cruelly to women, "who have no defence but their
tears, and who, on account of their ' *imbécilité et foi-
blesse*' should be humanely treated," and that if such
cruelties were continued, he could neither assist nor
favour them in the war ; so seeing that Champlain
was seriously displeased, " Captain Yroquet" promised
in future to spare the women, and only torment the
men ! On the following day, about three o'clock, they
arrived before the enemy's fort, and commenced skirmishing, driving him into his entrenchments ; after
which the "allies" withdrew out of the enemy's
sight, which seems to have angered Champlain extremely, moving him " to use and say rude and angry
words to incite them to do their duty," not according
to their councils, but in conformity with his notions.
He proposed to construct a " cavallier," a sort of high
platform, to overlook the enemy's palisades, in which
five or six arquebusiers being placed would soon dis-
lodge the foe ; also " mantelets," or large shields, to
protect them from arrows or stones. This being
done, they attacked the fort, his arquebusiers doing
great execution ; but his allies seconded him so
badly, making all kinds of blunders, that, after three
hours combat, two of their chiefs and about fifteen
of their men being wounded, and Champlain himself
hurt in the leg and knee by arrows, they withdrew,
in spite of all his remonstrances, and to his great indignation and disgust, saying, that when the five
hundred promised men should arrive, they would at-

tack the enemy again. The skirmishing continued
till the 9th, in which the enemy seems to have had
the best of it, as Champlain and his men were always
obliged to bring off their friends, the enemy retreat-
ing at sight of them, dreading their firearms, "urging,
by firm persuasion, that we ought not to mix in their
quarrels," which was perfectly true. Seeing that the
five hundred promised warriors did not arrive, the
allies resolved on retreat, carrying off Champlain in
a sort of basket on a man's back, "so tied and ham-
pered," says he, "that I lost patience, and as soon as
I had strength to support myself, I got out of that
prison, or rather, of that Gehenna!" On their way
back, they hunted a great deal, the savages being
better, according to his notions, at that sport than at
fighting. Champlain's explorings were very nearly
being here ended, as one day having followed a curious
bird too eagerly, he lost himself in the woods, and
wandered about for three days and nights, subsisting
on such game as he met with ; at last he resolved to
follow the course of some river or brook on the
chance of its leading him to the river on whose banks
the Indians were to encamp. Fortunately, he succeeded, and joined them in safety, but almost exhausted. They then all started on their return to
the village (Cahiagué), where they arrived on the
23rd.

After recruiting his strength, Champlain resolved
on visiting, during the winter, the tribes and country which the summer and the war had prevented his
exploring. He accordingly started on the 17th of

January (1616) for that purpose, but when he had arrived at the " Pisirinii" nation (Nipissing), he heard that a violent quarrel had broken out between his friends, the Algenquins, and their allies, which determined him to retrace his steps immediately, and endeavour to arrange the matter in dispute. He got back to the village on the 15th of February, and managed with great difficulty, by dint of persuasion, to patch up a sort of hollow truce, the Algenquins retiring to their own village, "saying they would no more winter there."

During the four or five months that he remained in the Indian territory, Champlain diligently examined the country, and studied the manners, customs, mode of life, ceremonies, and form of the assemblies of the natives, all of which he describes in his usual forcible and plain style. He left Cahiagué on the 20th May, and accompanied by many of the Indians arrived, after forty days journey, at Sault St. Louis, where he found Du Pont Gravé, who had just arrived from France with two ships, and who had despaired of again seeing him, having been told by some natives that he was dead. From thence he proceeded to the main settlement at Quebec. After three days sojourn there he went on to Tadoussac, and from thence embarked with Du Pont Gravé on the 3rd of August. On the 10th September, 1616, he arrived at Honfleur, " where," he says, " we rendered thanks and praises to God for having preserved us from the many perils and hazards to which we had been exposed, and for having brought us back

g

in safety to our country ; to Him, then, be glory and honour for ever ! So be it."

In 1617 Champlain again visited his colony, where he found all in a prosperous condition ; he therefore returned to France in the fall of the year, his presence in Paris being apparently more required than in Quebec, from the cabals, intrigues, and suits in which the company was continually engaged. The difficulties were materially increased by the pretensions of the States of Brittany to liberty of trade with New France, and which had been ratified by the Royal Council ; but Champlain bestired himself so actively, and pressed the associates to action so strongly, that the permission was withdrawn, and the Bretons prohibited from the traffic without the consent of the company.

In the year 1618 Champlain continued to urge the associates to greater activity and exertion, advising them to send out more men and materials than by their articles they were strictly bound to do, as the troubles which existed in France prevented the king from detaching any men for that service. The colony would otherwise languish, and the advantages they had already gained would be lost. The company objected, the unsettled and changeable state of affairs in France, and that which had happened to Mons. de Monts might well happen to them also ; but Champlain shewed them that matters were much changed, and the cases widely different, that Mons. de Monts was but a private gentleman, who had not influence enough to oppose hostility in the council of his ma-

jesty; but now the company had a prince of the
blood as chief and protector, who was viceroy of the
country to boot, and who could defend them against
all and every one, always under the king's good pleasure. By dint of perseverance and solicitation he
prevailed on the associates to assemble, and come to
an agreement as to the number of persons and the
necessary supplies which should be sent out. And a
curious and interesting list it is, compared with the
requirements of modern Quebec.

" List of persons to be sent to, and supported at,
the settlement of Quebec for the year 1619:—

" There shall be eighty persons, including the chief,
three Recollets Fathers, clerks, officers, workmen, and
labourers.

" Every two persons shall have a mattress, a paill-
asse, two blankets, three pair of new sheets, two coats
each, six shirts, four pair of shoes, and one capote.

" For the arms:—Forty musquets, with their ban-
daliers, twenty-four pikes, four arquebuses à rouet
(wheel-lock) of four to five feet, one thousand pounds
of fine powder, one thousand pounds of powder for
cannon, six thousand pounds of lead, and a match-
stump.

" For the men, a dozen scythes with their handles,
hammers, and other tools; twelve reaping-hooks,
twenty-four spades, twelve picks, four thousand pounds
of iron, two barrels of steel, ten tons of lime (none
having been then found in this country), ten thousand curved, or twenty thousand flat tiles, ten thousand
bricks to build an oven and chimneys, two mill-stones

(the kind of stone fit for that purpose was not discovered till some years afterwards).

" For the service of the table of the chief:—Thirty-
six dishes, as many bowls and plates, six saltcellars,
six ewers, two basins, six pots of six pints each, six
pints, six chopines (about half a pint), six demy-
septiers (about two gallons), the whole of pewter;
two dozen tablecloths, twenty-four dozen napkins.

" For the kitchen:—A dozen of copper boilers
(saucepans [?]) six pair andirons, six fryingpans, six
gridirons.

" Shall also be taken out—Two bulls of one year
old, heifers, and as many sheep as convenient; all
kinds of seeds for sowing.

" The commander of the settlement shall have
charge of the arms and ammunition which are ac-
tually there, and of those which shall afterwards be
sent, so long as he shall be in command: and the
clerk or factor who shall reside there shall take charge
of all merchandise, as well as of the furniture and
utensils of the company, and shall send a regular
account of them, signed by him, by the ships.

" Also shall be sent, a dozen mattresses complete,
like those of families, which shall be kept in the magazine for the use of the sick and wounded, etc., etc.

" Signed at Paris the 21st day of December, 1618,
and compared with the original (on paper) by the
undersigned natives, in the year 1619, the 11th day
of January.

" GUERREAU.
" FORCY."

This list was laid by Champlain before the Council of State, which highly approved of it, acknowledging the zeal and goodwill of the company, and refusing to listen to other proposals made by three of their opponents of Brittany, La Rochelle, and St. Jean de Luz. " There was also great talk," says Champlain, " of augmenting the population, which nevertheless came to nothing. The year passed away and nothing was done, nor in the following year either ; so that people began again to cry out and abuse the society, which made great promises, but performed nothing." It appears that some of the associates were of the " pretended Reformed religion," who, at heart, were strongly opposed to the Roman Catholic religion being implanted in the settlement. From this there arose so many divisions and broils, that what one party desired, the other would not listen to ; so that what with their intestine discord and the prosecution of the Rochellois, who were continually infringing on their privileges, the unfortunate company was in a state of confusion, becoming daily " worse confounded."

However, the company having obtained other decisions of the council in their favour, made fresh preparations, and got a vessel in readiness ; then set about quarrelling with Champlain, who was getting ready to sail with his family, saying, that they had advised together ; that the Sieur du Pont-Gravé should have the command in the settlement over their people ; and that he, Champlain, should employ himself in making discoveries, which was his special business, and which he had engaged to do. "In one word," he says, "they thought to keep the government to themselves, and establish a sort of republic of their own, making use of the commission of his majesty to accomplish their own ends, without anybody being able to control them." All this was done at the instigation of Boyer, before-mentioned, who, in all this chicanery, lived by the discords which he fomented. But the associates reckoned without their host. "They no longer considered their articles towards the king, Monseigneur le Prince, and me," writes Champlain, "and they esteem as nothing the contracts and promises which they have signed." So he wrote first to the company, and then went to Rouen (the chief seat of the company), with all his followers; there he produced their articles, and showed them that, as lieutenant of the prince, he had the right to command the settlement, and all the people there, or who might be sent, saving their chief clerk and people of the magazine, so far as trading affairs went; and as for discoveries, they were not to make laws for him; that he should set about them whenever circumstances should seem to him propitious, as he had done before; and that he was not obliged to do anything that was not in the articles, and they said nothing about discoveries. As for Du Pont-Gravé, he was his friend, and he respected him as a father; but that he would not suffer that which by right belonged to him (Champlain) to be given to another; that the pains, risks, and fortunes of life which he had incurred in the discoveries of lands and people, of which they derived the benefit, had gained him the honours which he possessed; that Du Pont-Gravé and he had always lived together in good friendship, and he wished to continue on the same terms; but he would not make the voyage, save with the same authority as before. Moreover, he would render the company liable for all expenses, damages, and interests that might be occasioned by delay; "and upon that," he adds, " I presented to them this letter from his majesty:—

"BY THE KING.

" Dear and well-beloved:—On the report made to us that there has hitherto been bad management in the establishment of the families and workmen sent to the settlement of Quebec, and other places of New France; We write to you this letter, to declare to you our desire that all things should proceed better in future; and to tell you, that it will give us pleasure that you should assist, as much as you conveniently can, the Sieur Champlain in the things requisite and necessary for the execution of the commands which he has received from us, to choose experienced and trusty men to be employed in the discovery, inhabiting, cultivating, and sowing the lands; and do all the works which he shall judge necessary for the establishment of the colonies which we desire to plant in the said country, for the good of the service and the use of our subjects; without, however, on account of the said discoveries and settlements, your factors, clerks, and agents in the traffic of peltry, being troubled or hindered in any way whatever

during the term which we have granted you. And
fail not in this, for such is our pleasure. Given at
Paris the 12th day of March, 1618.

(Signed)   " Louis.

(And below)   " Potier."

This letter, it might be supposed, would have settled
the matter, but the associates were stiff-necked ; so
Champlain made his protest and proceeded to Paris.
The vessel sailed without him, and Du Pont-Gravé
commanded, and wintered that year at the settlement,
while Champlain pleaded his rights before the king
and the Council of State.   " Nous voilà à chicaner,"
says he ; and with his characteristic activity and
energy, he followed the council to Tours, and, after
many and long debates, obtained a judgment, ordering
that he should have the command, not only at Quebec, but over all other settlements in New France,
and prohibiting the company from troubling or inter-
fering with him in the functions of his charge, under
penalty of damages, fines, expenses, etc. ; " and which
judgment," he adds, " I caused to be signified to the
associates in full Exchange at Rouen: they threw
the blame on Boyer, saying they had not consented,
but I knew better."   About this time Monseigneur
the Prince de Condé, with the king's permission, resigned the viceroyalty of New France to the Duc de
Montmorency, high-admiral of France, who seems to
have paid a round sum for the honour.[1]   Champlain

[1] In the beginning of 1620, the Duke de Montmorency was
created viceroy and lieutenant-general of New France and the
neighbouring islands and coasts, from Florida along the sea coast

was continued in the lieutenancy of the country, and
was ordered by the new viceroy to proceed to Quebec, to fortify himself there as well as he could, and
to let him know all that should occur, so that he
might take order accordingly. Monsieur Dolu,
Grand Audiencier of France, an able and well-
meaning man, was named intendant of the province,
" who," says Champlain, " burned with ardour to do
something for the advancement of the glory of God,
the good of the country, and to place our society in a
better position to do well than heretofore. I saw
him on the matter, and gave him a memoir for his
instruction."

Champlain accordingly left Paris with his family,
and everything necessary for the voyage, but at Honfleur the company, grievously annoyed at the over-
throw of their plans, again made some difficulties
about the command which he was to exercise. He
immediately wrote to the viceroy and to the new intendant, Monsieur Dolu, who sent instantly peremp-
tory notice to the associates, " that the king and
governor had determined that Champlain should
have the entire and absolute command in the colony,
and over all and everything in it, excepting always
their mere merchandise, of which their people might
dispose ; and if they would not obey the orders of his
majesty, Champlain was to stop their ships till the

to the Arctic circle ; to the west, from Newfoundland to the Great
Lake, called the Freshwater Sea (Lake Superior), with all the lands
adjoining the rivers which flow into the St. Lawrence, or Great
River of Canada ; the ports of Tadoussac and of Quebec, etc., etc.

h

said orders were executed ;" which at last brought them to their senses.

At the same time the king did Champlain the honour to write to him, with his own hand, the following letter.

" Champlain,—Having been informed of the commands which you have received from my cousin, the Duke of Montmorency, admiral of France, and my viceroy in New France, to proceed to the said country and be his lieutenant, and care for all that shall present itself for the good of my service, I have been pleased to write you this letter to assure you, that the services that you may render me on this occasion will be very agreeable to me, above all if you maintain the said country in its obedience to me, causing the people there to live, as much as you can, in conformity with the laws of my kingdom, and taking requisite care for the Catholic religion, in order, by that means, to attract the Divine benediction on you, which will cause your undertakings and actions to succeed, to the glory of God, whom I pray to have you in His holy keeping.

" Louis.

(And below)   " Brulart.

" Written at Paris, the 7th day of May 1620."

In the course of May 1620, Champlain at last again set sail for New France with his family, and after being nearly two months at sea, cast anchor in July opposite the mill of Baudé, about a league from Tadoussac, where, as usual, his first care was to return thanks to God for the preservation of himself

and his family, who had suffered much from the
perils of a bad voyage. He found there a vessel, on
board of which was his wife's brother, the Sieur
Boullé, who was greatly surprised at seeing his sister,
marvelling how she had ventured to pass the dangerous sea. Champlain also learned that the old
opponents of the company, the Rochelle people, had
sent two vessels, of seventy and eighty-five tons re-
spectively, to trade, in spite of the king's prohibition;
that they had obtained a great quantity of peltry and
other merchandise, and, what was worse, had supplied the natives with firearms and powder and ball.

Champlain is very bitter against the Rochellois
(who were Protestants), calling them " meschans lar-
rons"—wicked rascals, " who came into the country
to suborn the savages, and hold very pernicious and
bad discourse about our religion, in order to render
us odious!"

On the 11th of July Champlain left Tadoussac for
Quebec, with his family, three missionaries, whom he
had brought out with him, his brother-in-law, Boullé,
and Guers, his commissary, and immediately on arriving he proceeded to the chapel to give thanks to
God. On the morrow, after mass, " a sermon of
exhortation" was preached by a Recollet father, ex-
plaining to all their duty towards the king and the
Duke de Montmorency, and to Champlain as their
lieutenant; after which Guers, the commissary, read
publicly the king's and the viceroy's commissions,
appointing Champlain to the sole command of the
colony; " which being done, every one cried ' Vive

le roy,' the cannon was fired in token of joy, and thus I took possession of the settlement and the country."

Champlain, thus fairly installed in his government, immediately bestirred himself to bring matters to some state of order, which, during his absence in France, had fallen into confusion and neglect,—the buildings almost in ruins, the gardens unenclosed, and the land badly and scantily cultivated. In a short time, however, the houses were rapidly and solidly restored, and the settlement resumed an appearance of progress and prosperity. His next care was to erect a fort on the heights which commanded the narrowest part of the river, notwithstanding the objections which were made by the associates and their agents. Guers, the commissary, was sent with six men to Trois Rivières, where Du Pont Gravé and the clerks of the company were, to see how affairs were going on in that quarter. The change of viceroy and alteration of the arrangements were so displeasing to some of the company's people, that Du Pont Gravé resolved on returning to France with some of the disaffected, and Champlain remained to govern his little colony, which then consisted of sixty persons, men, women, priests, and children, of whom ten men were employed in the religious seminary, but at the expense of the mission. He continued to occupy himself with building and fortifying with his accustomed activity, but he was not permitted to remain long untroubled. In the spring of 1621 a vessel arrived from France commanded by a Captain de May, who brought letters announcing a complete change in the intentions of the viceroy and in the affairs of the company, and which soon converted the tranquillity of the settlement into something approaching to open rebellion.

The letter of the viceroy was as follows.

" Monsieur Champlain,—For many reasons I have thought fit to exclude the former company of Rouen and St. Malo from the trade with New France, and to assist you and provide you with everything necessary, I have chosen the Sieurs de Caen, uncle and nephew, and their associates; one is a good merchant, the other a good naval captain, who can aid you well, and make the authority of the king respected in my government. I recommend you to assist him and those who shall apply to you on his part, so as to maintain them in the enjoyment of the articles which I have granted them. I have charged the Sieur Dolu, intendant of the affairs of the country, to send you a copy of the treaty by the first voyage, so that you may know to what they are bound, in order that they may execute their engagement, as, on my part, I desire to perform what I have promised. I have taken care to preserve your appointments, as I believe you will continue to serve the king well. Your most affectionate and perfect friend,

" MONTMORENCY.

" From Paris, 2nd February, 1621."

The king also honoured him with a flattering letter in these terms :

" Champlain,—I have perceived by your letters of

the 15th of August, with what affection you work at
your establishment, and for all that regards the good
of my service; for which, as I am thankful to you,
so I shall have pleasure in recognizing it to your
advantage whenever the occasion shall offer; and I
have willingly granted some munitions of war, which
were required to give you better means to subsist
and to continue in that good duty, which I promise
myself from your care and fidelity.

" Louis.

" Paris, this 24th February, 1621.

The letters of the intendant, M. Dolu, informed
him that he must stop the trading of the clerks of
the old company and seize all the merchandise, on
account of the claims which the king and Monsieur
de Montmorency had against them for not having
fulfilled their engagement of sending out people and
" material," to which, by their articles, they were
bound.   That, as for the Sieur de Caen, although he
was of the contrary religion, yet he gave hopes of
becoming a Catholic, but that Champlain was not to
suffer the practice of his actual faith either by sea or
land.   De Caen wrote that he had arrived with two
vessels, well armed and equipped with every necessary, and was the bearer of letters from the viceroy
and M. Dolu, enjoining Champlain to change or do
nothing without communicating to him (De Caen),
who had force enough with him, being also furnished with orders in his favour, to seize the ships
and merchandise of the old company, and in the
mean time Champlain was to take charge of the

peltry, etc., till they could be legally seized and taken.

The clerks of the company, however, were not disposed to give up their property so easily, unless Champlain could shew some letter or order of the king to that effect, which he could not do. He promised them not to make any innovation until De Caen should arrive with the commands of his majesty, which must be obeyed, and in the meantime Captain De May should not be allowed to trade. This latter was despatched by Champlain to inform De Caen of what had occurred, and of the state in which matters were, and to beg him to send some men to reinforce him. De May returned on the 3rd June, bringing ten men with him, and the intelligence of the arrival of Du Pont Gravé from France in a vessel of one hundred and fifty tons, and sixty-five men, accompanied by all the clerks of the old company. This singularly complicated matters, and obliged Champlain to act with great circumspection, lest the people of the old company, being in the majority, should turn the tables and seize the vessel and cargo of De May. So he placed his brother-in-law, Boullé, with De May and sixteen men, and plenty of provisions, arms, and ammunition, in the little fort which he was building; continuing the works, also, as fast as possible, so as to be in a fit state of defence. "And then," says Champlain, "Nous parlerons à cheval!" He removed into the village or town of the settlement, which was protected by the fort, giving De May certain orders how to act in case of need.

On the 7th June the old company's clerks arrived, wherefore Champlain made his men stand to their arms as a measure of precaution, and after some debate, as De Caen had not arrived or forwarded his commission, and as Champlain had no positive orders to the contrary, they were allowed to proceed with their goods up the river to trade. The clerks then asked for arms, and wished that the peltry already in the magazine should be given up to them; but to both Champlain demurred, saying that as they had not brought him any provisions or munitions for the settlement, he must keep both weapons and skins, in order to defend himself, or exchange the peltry for food in case of need.   He thus with great prudence kept matters in equilibrium for the moment, sending again to De Caen to hasten his arrival with rein- forcements and the orders of the king.

On the 13th, Du Pont Gravé arrived at Quebec, with goods and twelve men. Champlain told him the arrangement he had made with the clerks, on which Du Pont Gravé continued his route to Trois Rivières to trade with the Indians, confiding in Champlain's promise to do justice to all till the king's commands should arrive. De Caen, on the 15th, wrote to Champlain to go to him at Tadoussac (which he then refused), and to give notice to the Indians of his arrival, and warn them that they were not to trade with any others. To make the confusion complete, on the 17th, Champlain received letters stating that the old company had obtained a judg- ment authorizing them to trade for the year 1621, conjointly with the new company (De Caen's). As De Caen did not arrive, and the departure of the clerks, Du Pont Gravé, and his people, for the upper part of the river had, for the present, removed all danger from the fort and settlement, Champlain resolved to go down to Tadoussac, leaving De May in command. On his arrival he had long " discourse" with De Caen, wherein he gave him very good counsel as to the obedience to be given to the orders of the king and governor; which De Caen promised, but wished the peltry, etc., which had been already collected to be delivered to him. Champlain declined, unless he could produce specific orders to that effect, which De Caen averred that he had, but would not produce; and getting angry, and consequently obstinate, declared that, if his wish was not complied with, he would seize Du Pont Gravé's ship, by force, if necessary. Champlain replied, that in that case he should take the vessel under his protection and safeguard, so that the forms of justice might be preserved, and that De Caen, having superior force, might afterwards do as he pleased on his own responsibility; and therefore sent to take possession of the ship. De Caen then also sent a force to occupy the vessel, declaring he would punish those who should resist; on which Champlain, under protest of the employment of " force majeure", withdrew, thus preserving his prerogative while matters were in suspense, without having recourse to violence.

But while the partisans of the two companies were

thus contending for the trade, neither making much progress, one of Champlain's abominations, a little Rochellois vessel, came in quietly, and carried off great part of the object in dispute—trading with the natives, selling powder and guns and warlike stores, and packing up peltry under their very noses; and when at last Champlain and De Caen in great indignation sent to catch the interloper— the bird had flown. De Caen, however, seems to have gained but little by the great fuss that he made, for after sending in some arms and ammunition to the settlement (which, by the way, Champlain plainly hints were not by any means all that had been sent), and settled his affairs for a time, he left for France on the 18th August, and Du Pont Gravé shortly followed him, leaving Champlain once more to finish building his fort and rule his little colony in peace.

The end of all this turmoil was, that the rival companies " amalgamated" in the following year.

Being now tranquil, and free to occupy himself without interruption for the good of the settlement and the country, Champlain passed the year 1622 and the following in building—not forgetting his favourite fort—in clearing land, establishing fisheries, and in strengthening and consolidating the trade. He also made peace between the friendly tribes of Indians and their old enemies the Iroquois, and having assured the good order of the colony, and his fort being nearly finished, he resolved to return to France for a time with his family. He accordingly embarked at Tadoussac on the 21st of August, 1624,

and on the 1st of October entered the harbour of
Dieppe. After a two days repose he proceeded with
his suite to St. Germains, to give a report to the king
and the viceroy of his proceedings, and of the events
which had occurred during his four years absence.
He found the two companies again at loggerheads,
and their continued disputes so worried the Duke de
Montmorency, that he gave up the viceroyalty—"qui
luy rompuist plus la teste, que ses affaires plus im-
portantes"—to the Duke de Ventadour (for " a consideration," however, according to the practice of the
time), who, " animated by the zeal and affection
which he had to see the glory of God flourish in
those barbarous lands," sent out six Jesuits in the
following year at his own expense.[1]

The new viceroy also appointed Champlain his

---

[1] It was not so much the worry of the Duke de Montmorency,
as the intrigues of the Jesuits, which induced him to give up, or
rather sell, the viceroyalty. The whole negotiation is explained
in the *Hist. Canadensis* of the Jesuit Du Creux (or Creuxius, as
he styles himself), Paris, 1664. The Duke de Ventadour was
very devout, had even taken holy orders, and was quite in the
Jesuits' hands : they wishing to get, or rather strengthen their
footing in Canada, after many expedients, settled the matter as
follows: "Viâ certa demum hæc judicata; Pro rege Novæ Franciæ
dignitatem à Duce Montmorantio, coëmeret Ventadorius. . . . Nec
mora, agit continuò cum Montmorantio Ventadorius; cum eoque
brevi decidit in Librarum Turonensium (Livres Tournois) centum
millia, et quod excurrit hæc tam grandi pecunia pene profundendiâ
illustrissime testatus, quam sibi cordi, Canadensis res esset."—
Lib. i, p. 4. One hardly knows which most to admire, the simplicity of the worthy " Creuxius" in thus letting out the secret, or
the abominable Latin in which he narrates the whole affair.

lieutenant in New France, and he remained in Paris partly to give the duke some insight into the affairs of the colony, partly for his private affairs; the Sieur De Caen also received a commission (or had it renewed), from the new governor, and prepared to continue his voyages; but he seems to have had a taste for disputes and litigation, as he contrived to pick a quarrel with the united companies, in which, however, he got the better of them, and was permitted to send out vessels; one of the conditions being, " that the command should be given to a catholic."

The ships being ready to sail from Dieppe, Champlain, and his brother-in-law, Boullé, who had been named his lieutenant, embarked on the 15th April, 1626, on board of the *Catharine*, of two hundred and fifty tons; and after a tedious voyage of two months and six days, again landed in new France; finding Du Pont Gravé (who had returned in the previous year, and had been extremely ill during the winter), the missionaries, and all the people in good health, but almost reduced to extremity for want of provisions; and the buildings, etc., in nearly the same state as when he left.

Champlain here complains bitterly of the carelessness of the company in not providing sufficient supplies of provisions, and of the improvidence and carelessness of the people; as, but for his arrival, the colony would probably have been abandoned, from famine.

The cause assigned for the delay in finishing the dwellings and constructions planned by Champlain, previous to his departure was, that fully one half of the men were employed during two months and a half of the best part of the year, in collecting and bringing in forage for the cattle, which they were obliged to fetch from Cape Tourmente, quite eight leagues from the settlement. To obviate this difficulty, Champlain established a farm in a favourable spot at the foot of the said cape, where the cattle could remain at pasture, and but few men be required to look after them. He also appointed an overseer to stay there permanently, and take care that the labourers did not waste their time; and every week he paid a visit of inspection to the new establishment. Considering also that the fort which he had commenced was but small, that, by and bye, as the population increased, more soldiers would be required for the defence of the colony; and that " selon l'oyseau il fallait la cage,"—he resolved to make the " cage according to the bird," and pull down and enlarge it. He pushed on the works so that they might be in a fit state of defence in the spring; and erected two bastions, well flanked, to protect the land side, by which alone it could be approached, and only then with difficulty. In the autumn, he received news of an outbreak of his old acquaintances the Iroquois, who had slain five Dutchmen, being at war with the Mahiganathicoit (Mohicans), in whose country the Dutch were settled about the fortieth degree of latitude, "near to Virginia, where the Englishmen were established." His old friend, Du Pont Gravé, who seems to have been a martyr to the gout for some time past, resolved to return to France, and he little expected ever to see him again.

About this time Champlain suffered much anxiety on account of the insufficient supplies of provisions from France, which had become most necessary,—the people, notwithstanding their long sojourn in the country, depending chiefly on the arrival of the ships for support; he had even been obliged to send some families back to France, who, instead of working or cultivating the land, did nothing but hunt, and shoot, and fish, and amuse themselves from morning till night, being idle themselves and the cause of idleness in others. He notices (January, 1627) the death of one Hebert, " the first head of a family who lived by what he cultivated." The Missionaries seem to be making progress among the natives at this time, as the Reverend (Jesuit) Father Lallemand, " baptised a little savage of only ten or twelve days old," who was buried the next day in the cemetery of the settlement.

The winter of 1626-27 was very long and severe, the snow lying very deep and long on the ground, and the usual improvidence of the settlers causing provisions to run short. In the course of it, some of the Indian tribes, of the country inhabited by the Dutch, begged the assistance of Champlain's native allies, to make war against the Iroquois, who had killed twenty-five of their people (besides five of the Dutch) because they had refused them passage through their territory, to attack the " Loups," Indians with whom the said Iroquois were at feud.

The Algenquins and some other of the friendly tribes consented to the peace, which Champlain had with such difficulty made between his friends and the Iroquois, being broken to his great indignation: other tribes refused, without the consent of Champlain. He did all in his power to prevent the war, sending his brother-in-law, Boullé, with Emery De Caen, the nephew, to the rendezvous of the savages for that purpose, but to no avail; three Iroquois were taken prisoners and tormented, and the war commenced. Champlain thereupon hastened in person to the Indian camp, and with great difficulty prevailed on them to send back one of the prisoners, with presents, to propitiate the Iroquois and renew the peace. On his return to Quebec he there found, to his surprise, Du Pont Gravé just arrived, having returned to Canada at the solicitation of the elder De Caen (who was detained in France), notwithstanding his almost constant sufferings from the gout.

Champlain had returned but a few weeks to his post, when he received intelligence that "the ambassadors," who had been sent with the Iroquois prisoner, had all been murdered by the " Ouentanoronnons" (Hurons?), who were allies of the Iroquois. Among the envoys were one Pierre Magnan, a Frenchman, and a chief called " De Reconcilié." " The latter," says Champlain, " well deserved his death, for having massacred two of our men at Cape Tourmente; and Magnan, who was from the vicinity of Lisieux, had killed a man of that neighbourhood, and had been obliged to take refuge in New France. " See," he

continues, "how God sometimes chastises the men
who seek to avoid his justice in one way, and are
caught in another." All hope of peace was now at
an end, and Champlain was compelled to avenge the
death of his countryman, however unworthy, lest, by
passing over the affront, greater injury might follow;
so he prepared for hostilities, and his Indian friends
recommended tormenting a wretched prisoner whom,
at Champlain's intercession, they had hitherto spared,
with more than usual barbarity, roasting him by a
slow fire, and "every one carried off a piece of him,
which they ate!"

Affairs also became more complicated from the
old complaint—scarcity of provisions, the English
having taken one of the company's ships; and by the
resistance of the associates to the viceroy's orders
and regulations, refusing to contribute to the erection
of the fort, and not troubling themselves about king
or governor, or how matters went on, provided they
received their profits of about forty per cent. It
was evident that "they who govern the purse could
do, and would do at pleasure." Champlain could do
nothing, save to write an account of the state of
things to the viceroy, that he might act accordingly,
and work at his fort and other buildings of the
settlement.[1]

---

[1] Scarcity of provisions. "Nec minus animo Camplenius ange-
batur, Galli remanebant quinque et quinquaginta, quibus in istis
angustiis difficultatibusque, victum quotidianum tandiu præbere
haud facillimum merito putabatur, etc."—Du Creux, *Hist. Canadensis*, lib. i, p. 13.

On the 20th of September, 1627, some scouts of the Indians informed Champlain that a great number of Iroquois were on their way to attack him, to which he replied, " that he was glad of it, but did not believe the news, as they had only courage to attack sleeping men"; and, in fact, some months later, two of his men, conducting cattle from the farm at Cape Tourmente to Quebec, were murdered during their sleep, not by the Iroquois, but by his own allies. Champlain, thoroughly roused at this treachery, peremptorily demanded that the murderers should be given up, and declared that, till that was done, he should keep three of the savages as hostages; the Indians requested three days, that they might endeavour to discover the assassin; and, in the mean time, Champlain kept on his guard, taking every precaution against surprise or open attack, the affair having now become very serious, as the settlement was completely surrounded by the tribes.

The Indians, after the expiration of the three days, sent word that they could not find the murderer, but as proof of good faith, and to make amends, offered to give Champlain three young girls, to be brought up and treated as he should please; " a thing never before known," says Champlain, " as our surgeon and many there wished to take young girls and marry them, but the savages would never consent."[1]   After

---

[1] Three young girls. " Accessere sub extremum Januarium virgunculæ indigenæ tres, ultro præter morem, oblutæ à parentibus... partem metu, ne Gallorum duorum cædem, quos Barbari aliquot dormientes, recens, per summam inhumanitatem oppres-

consultation with Du Pont Gravé, (who, while thinking that the arrangement might be good, opposed
the reception of the girls, on account of the scarcity
of food,[1]) the girls were accepted; but on condition,
that Champlain should nevertheless be at liberty to
seek for the murderer, and punish him when found.
These " virgunculæ " were destined to be a source of
considerable trouble and pain to Champlain, as will
shortly be seen.

The colony continued tolerably flourishing and
quiet, with the exception of the squabbles of the
associates of the Company (now become apparently
habitual) among themselves, with the viceroy and
all authorities, and with everybody in short, and of
the usual deficiency of provisions; till the month of
July, 1628, when Champlain received a surprise of
quite a different kind, and far more serious than any
of his previous troubles and difficulties.   On the 9th
July, two of his men, coming from Cape Tourmente,
told him that, according to the report of a savage,
(who, on the same day, confirmed the news,) six
ships had arrived at Tadoussac, and that a certain
Captain Michel of Dieppe was the chief commander
for the Sieur De Caen.   At first Champlain thought
that this commander was a certain Michel with whom
De Caen was associated in the fishery at Gaspey;
but on reflection, it seemed little probable, as Michel
was not a fit person for such a command, and that

serant, Camplenius gravius ulcisceretur, etc."—Du Creux, *Hist.
Canadensis*, lib. i, p. 13.

   [1] " In summâ inopiâ, pernegante Pontio·Gravæo !"—Du Creux.

six vessels were an extrordinary number for the trade or fishery, so that some great change must have taken place in general affairs. Champlain therefore desired a young Greek, who acted as interpreter, to disguise himself as an Indian, and to proceed with two natives in a canoe to reconnoitre. Champlain was in great doubt, fearing, what he had often apprehended, that an enemy would arrive, and that the aforesaid ships were hostile: he therefore took order both at the fort and settlement so as to receive the enemy properly, if needed.

About an hour after the departure of the Greek, he suddenly returned accompanied by two canoes which were hastening to the settlement, in one of which was Foucher, the superintendent of the farm at Cape Tourmente, who told Champlain that he had just escaped from the English, who had taken him prisoner with three of his men, a woman, and a little girl, whom they had carried off to a barque which was at anchor off the Cape, having killed all the beasts they had need of, and burned the remainder in the stables; they had also set fire to two small houses, and ravaged and pillaged everything, even the head-gear of the little girl; they had then re-embarked in haste, fearing to be pursued; "which," says Champlain, "assuredly they would have been, if the savages, who all knew of their arrival, had informed us of it; but, like perfidious traitors as they are, they not only concealed this unpleasant news, but spread the report that the strangers were our own people, and that we were not to be anxious

about them." It appeared that the enemy had
arrived at Cape Tourmente an hour or so before daylight, and sent about fifteen soldiers ashore, thinking
to surprise Foucher and his people asleep; but on
approaching the habitation, Foucher met them, asking, " who they were and what they wanted ?" They
replied in French that they were friends: " Do you
not recollect us? We were here last year, and we
are now sent by Monseigneur the Cardinal and Monseigneur de Roquemont with intelligence; in passing
we wished to see you." With these civilities and
gentle words they saluted, gradually surrounding
Foucher and his men, who were presently astonished
at being seized and made prisoners, as before related,
" the treacherous savages having told them of the
state in which we were." Champlain, at this con-
firmation of his fears, immediately set everybody to
work at making intrenchments around the little
town, and stockades on the ramparts of the fort
(which was not finished for want of workmen), appointing every man his post, to which he was to
hasten when required.

On the next day, the 10th of July, about three in
the afternoon, a boat was seen approaching the settlement, which, from its manœuvres, seemed to make
for the St. Charles river, either to disembark men
or to set fire to the house of the mission, which was
there situated, or else, that the crew did not know
the right channel to the town. Champlain sent some
arquebusiers to reconnoitre, who found that the supposed enemies were the men with the woman and

girl who had just been taken prisoners, with six Basques, who had also been captured by the English. One of the latter was bearer of a letter from the English "General" at Tadoussac, to this effect:—
" Messieurs,—I give you notice that I have received a commission from the king of Great Britain, my honoured lord and master, to take possession of the countries of Canada and Acadia, and for that purpose eighteen ships have been dispatched, each taking the route ordered by His Majesty. I have already seized the habitation at Miscare, and all boats and pinnaces on that coast, as well as those of Tadoussac, where I am presently at anchor. You are also informed that, among the vessels that I have seized, there is one belonging to the new company, commanded by a certain Norot, which was coming to you with provisions and goods for the trade. The Sieur De la Tour was also on board, whom I have taken into my ship. I was preparing to seek you, but thought it better to send boats to destroy and seize your cattle at Cape Tourmente; for I know that, when you are straitened for supplies, I shall the more easily obtain my desire, which is, to have your settlement; and in order that no vessels shall reach you, I have resolved to remain here till the end of the season, in order that you may not be re-victualled. Therefore see what you wish to do,— if you intend to deliver up the settlement or not, for, God aiding, sooner or later I must have it. I would desire, for your sake, that it should be by courtesy rather than by force, to avoid the blood

which might be spilt on both sides. By surrendering
courteously, you may be assured of all kind of contentment, both for your persons and for your property, which, on the faith that I have in Paradise,
I will preserve as I would my own, without the least
portion in the world being diminished. The Basques,
whom I send you, are men of the vessels that I have
captured, and they can tell you the state of affairs
between France and England, and even how matters
are passing in France, touching the new company[1]
of this country. Send me word what you desire to
do; and if you wish to treat with me about this
affair, send me a person to that effect, whom, I
assure you, I will treat with all kind of attention,
and I will grant all reasonable demands that you
may desire in resolving to give up the settlement.

"Waiting your reply, I remain, Messieurs,

"Your affectionate servant,

"DAVID QUER.

"On board the 'Vicaille' (?) this 18th of July,
1628 (old style), and addressed to 'Monsieur Champlain, Commandant at Quebec.'"

---

[1] On the 29th April, 1627, another company for the trade with
New France, to the exclusion of all previous associations, and
styled the Company of the Hundred Associates, was organized,
and the articles settled and signed, under the especial patronage
and influence of the Cardinal de Richelieu; and on the 29th June
the Duke de Ventadour resigned the post of viceroy of New France,
in consideration of the sum of seventy thousand livres, which the
President de Lauzun promised him on the part of the king. The
"Great Cardinal" had been already invested in 1626 with the direc-
tion of all naval affairs, under the title of Grand Master and Super-

This logical, precise, and " affectionate" letter being read, " We concluded," says Champlain, " that if he wished to see us he had better come, and not threaten from such a distance;" so replied in equally polite terms to the purport, " That he did not in the least doubt the fact of Quer (or Keith) having the commission of his king, as great princes always select men of brave and generous courage," acknowledging the intelligence of the capture of Norot and De la Tour, and also the truth of the observation that, the more provisions there were in a fortress the better it could hold out, still it could be maintained with but little, provided good order were kept; therefore, being still provided with grain, maize, beans, and peas, (besides what the country could furnish,) which his soldiers loved as well as the finest corn in the world, by surrendering the fort in so good a condition, he should be unworthy to appear before his sovereign, and should deserve chastisement before God and men. He was sure that Quer would respect him much more for defending himself, than for abandoning his charge, without first making trial of the English guns and batteries;" concluding, that he should expect his attack, and oppose, as well as he could, all attempts that might be made against the place; and signing, " Your affectionate servant, Champlain."

intendant of Navigation and Commerce, those of admiral and vice-admiral of France being suppressed. His first care was to put down the rival companies, and take the trade into his own hands; the next, to get rid of the Jesuits, and their tool the Duke de Ventadour.

This courteous, but decided, and, under the circumstances, chivalrous answer, was given to the Basques to deliver to the English commander, who, finding that Champlain was determined to hold out, and thinking that the settlement was better provided with provisions and stores than it really was, contented himself with burning all the boats and vessels at Tadoussac, and set sail again to look for ships along the coast; and well it was for Champlain that he did so, as he writes, " Every man being reduced to seven ounces of peas a day, and only having about fifty pounds of gunpowder, hardly any matches or other commodities, if they had made their point, we could hardly have resisted them."

The English admiral or chief, David Quer, or Keith (most likely Kerr), was, it is said, a Calvinist of Dieppe, the son of a Scotchman, who had married there, and who had quitted France on account of the persecutions against the Protestants. It appears that De Caen, enraged at the privileges of the company of which he was the head being annulled, and himself excluded from the new company formed under the auspices of Cardinal Richelieu, betrayed the settlement, giving the English a full and complete account of the vessels employed, the number of men in the colony, its weak points, etc. Kerr had with him also a certain Jacques Michel, a Frenchman, from Dieppe, and a former associate of De Caen.[1]

---

[1] " Fauces illas, aditusque fluminis obsidebat jam aliquandiu David Kersius, Anglus, ab navibus, militibusque Rupemontio instructor... præmonitus pridem ab exulceratis Cadomianis (De

Some days afterwards a young man, of the name of Desdames, came to Quebec with ten men, bringing news of the arrival at Gaspey of the Sieur de Roquement, commanding the new company's ships, which were bringing stores, provisions, and workmen and their families for the colony. Champlain, whom the late surprise had rendered doubly cautious, asked for letters from De Roquement, before giving credence to this intelligence; surprised, moreover, that in such suspicious times, he had not written by his messenger, to say how affairs were going on in France, and tell him about this new company that had ousted De Caen and his partners, and of which Champlain knew nothing.[1] Desdames told him that he had left in such haste that De Roquement had not time to write, but in proof of the truth of his intelligence, produced a few lines from Father Lallemand, a Jesuit, who was on board De Roquement's vessel, saying that, in a short time, Champlain would

Caen), qui exclusos sese ab Novâ Franciâ, tantâ vel ignominiâ, vel rei familiaris jacturâ impotentissimé ferebant, de navium transmissarum numero, de Noyrotis actuario nominatim, de militum robore, de commeatu, de omnibus denique, quæ hostis incendere cupiditatem, vel stimulare diligentiam, vel cautionem munire posse videbantur."—De Creux, lib. i.

[1] Champlain, however, shortly after received a commission from the king, Louis XIII, appointing him commandant in New France under Cardinal Richelieu, ordering him also to take an inventory of all goods and property of every kind belonging to De Caen, and to have them valued; and also, to send without delay an account of the state of the settlement, the number of acres of cleared land, and plans of the fort and buildings, etc., for the deliberation of the royal council.

see them, if not prevented by the English, who were stronger than they were. Desdames also informed him that De Roquement intended to attack the English squadron at Tadoussac, and that on his route he had heard cannon, which made him think that the battle had commenced.

Champlain severely blamed the conduct of De Roquement in attacking the English, as, being sent for the sole purpose of succouring and revictualling the fort and settlement which were in want of almost every necessary, if he were beaten, he not only ruined himself but the country, leaving nearly a hundred men, women, and children to die of hunger, or abandon the fort and settlement to the first enemy that should present himself. On the contrary, the English being stronger in ships and men, he ought to have avoided them as much as possible. " The merit of a good captain," he exclaims, " is not in his courage alone; it ought to be accompanied by prudence, which causes him to be respected, being accompanied by many cunning stratagems and inventions; many have thus done much with little, and have rendered themselves glorious and redoubtable."

While waiting with impatience for news of the combat, " Nous mangions nos pois par compte," which short allowance greatly reduced the strength of the people, most of the men becoming feeble, and hardly able to work. " We were deprived of all," says Champlain; " even salt was wanting." His ingenuity, however, provided a partial remedy for the evil of eating the peas whole; he first had mortars made wherein the peas might be pounded to a coarse flour; but the labour required being considerable, he imagined that a hand-mill would be better, but there were no mill-stones; however, as by dint of seeking most things are to be found, his locksmith discovered stone fit for the purpose. " So that," Champlain writes, " this necessity made us find that which for twenty years had been deemed impossible." When the hand-mill was finished, every one brought his little supply of peas, which they received back in flour, and which, made into a kind of soup, " did us a great deal of good, and set us up better than we had been for some time." So with the addition of a small supply of eels, from time to time, from the Indians, who, by the bye, sold them very dear, he continued to rub on as best he might. The success of his hand-mill encouraged him to have water-mills erected during the winter, which would better relieve the people, and spare labour. He also sent out men to hunt in the winter, " as the savages did, but," he adds, indignantly, " they were not so honest as those people, as having taken a very large elk, they amused themselves with devouring it like ravenous wolves, without giving us any, save about twenty pounds; which made me reproach them for their gluttony, as I never had any provisions without sharing with them; but as they were men without honour or civility, so had they acted, and I sent them no more, occupying them with other things."

Champlain's difficulties and anxieties became daily

greater, as, with the utmost possible economy, the few remaining provisions would hardly last longer than the end of May, and if the annual ships with supplies were lost or taken by the English, they must all perish with hunger; so he resolved that, if the vessels did not arrive by the end of June, and the English should return as they had promised, to make the best terms he could and give up the fort, as the people could not otherwise subsist; and if neither the English nor the ships should arrive, to patch up, as well as he could, a little vessel of seven or eight tons, which had been left at Quebec as being good for nothing, and go to Gaspey, Miscou, and other places to the north, to try and get a passage for the greater part of the settlers, in the vessels which went there for the fishery, retaining in the settlement only such a number as might subsist on the grain which would be gathered in the following August from the lands of " Hebert " before mentioned, and of the " Fathers," who seemed to have taken care of themselves in all this necessity. " To exist till August," says he, " our resource would be to seek for herbs and roots, and try and catch fish." If he found that the little vessel could not be repaired, he determined to take with him as many men as possible and make war on some of the savage tribes who had aided the Iroquois; to force one of their villages and fortify it, so as to pass the rest of the summer, the autumn, and winter, rather than all die of hunger at the settlement, " hoping for better things in the spring."

While in this extreme tribulation, an Indian chief, of a tribe some eight days journey from Quebec, paid Champlain a visit for the purpose of soliciting his aid against the old foe, the Iroquois. Considering it an excellent opportunity for relieving the settlement of many surplus mouths, he agreed to help them as well as he could in that year if the vessels should not arrive, and, at any rate, in the next year he would join them with as many men as possible; at least he and his people would be fed, and if the English took possession of the settlement, his alliance with the Indians would enable him in due time to drive them out. With this promise the Indian chief departed highly pleased, and Champlain sent a confidential man to reconnoitre the enemy's country, giving his Indian friends instructions how to attack the Iroquois villages or forts till he could join them. He then sent a small boat to Gaspey to try and get some grain, and applied to " Father Joseph De la Roche," (he does not say of which mission, Jesuit or Recollet,) to know if he might hope for some supplies from their stock if the ships should not arrive; the worthy Father Joseph replied that, if it depended upon him, he would gladly consent, but that " Father Joseph Caron, the guardian, must be first applied to." Whether the said supplies were forthcoming does not appear; from the continuance, and even increase of suffering, it should seem not.

On the 20th of May, twenty Indian warriors, coming from Tadoussac, on their way to make war on the Iroquois, brought some account of the battle which had been fought between the English and French ships. Some men had been killed ; the Sieur De Roquement wounded in the foot, and the French vessels taken and carried into Gaspey ; the crews had been all put on board one of the ships to be sent to France, the officers kept as prisoners of war, and the English, after burning a " cache " of corn belonging to the Jesuits at Gaspey, had set sail for England.

About this time Champlain formed an alliance with an Indian chief named " Chomina," who greatly relieved his anxieties about future subsistence by promising to assist him, as much as possible, with provisions, and in case of need, against the English. Desdames also arrived from Gaspey, confirming the intelligence brought by the Indians of the total defeat and capture of the French ships, and that eight English vessels were cruising on the coast of Acadia.

On the 26th of June Champlain dispatched his brother-in-law, Boullé, with all who wished to leave the settlement, to Gaspey, with orders to seek a passage to France, by every possible means, charging him with letters for the king, the cardinal, the council of state, and the company, giving details of all that had passed, and of the strait to which he was reduced. Du Pont Gravé, who had remained at Quebec, was also desirous of returning, but on Champlain's representations of the difficulties and danger of life he would incur from his infirm state, in so hazardous a journey, he remained at the settlement, so tormented with the gout that he was almost constantly laid up.

When Boullé and his people had departed, Champlain employed those who remained in preparing the ground and sowing turnips against the winter, and, while awaiting the harvest, parties were sent every day to seek for roots, which occasioned great fatigue, having to go seven or eight leagues to find any, and even then hardly getting enough for bare subsistence. Some tried fishing, but with little success, "nets, lines, and hooks being wanting," and gunpowder so scarce, that he preferred suffering rather than use for hunting the little he had left, which was not more than thirty or forty pounds, and that very bad.

Every day also he was in expectation of the arrival of some Hurons with twenty Frenchmen, who had gone with them some time before to relieve the settlement a little—"pour nous soulager de nos pois" —as Champlain expresses it ; and these expected additions to the claims on the said "pois" gave him no small anxiety, "as we had nothing whatever to give them, unless they brought flour with them." He hoped that the Hurons would take them with them again, or that he could distribute them among other tribes near him ; but that was very uncertain. His troubles were, however, considerably relieved by his friend "Chomina offering to go to the Huron country to seek for flour," and, still more, by the arrival of one of his men whom he had sent to examine the country of the "Abenaquoit"(?) Indians, who gave him a full report of the rapids and other difficulties of the route thither, and, what was then better and more to the purpose, that the said "Abenaquoits" were very friendly, and had offered to take some of his people and keep them during the winter, or till he should receive supplies by the arrival of the ships or otherwise.

On the 17th of July, the Hurons and their French guests arrived, but bringing hardly any provisions, so that they were obliged to do as Champlain and his people did, " seek for roots that they might live." He deliberated about sending them to the friendly " Abenaquoits" to reside with them till the spring, " having no longer any hope," he touchingly adds, " of seeing either friends or enemies, the season being, to all appearance, past." The Hurons could only offer for sale two sacks of flour, one of which was bought by the Recollet fathers, the other by Du Pont Gravé. " As for me," says Champlain, " it was quite out of my power to have any, much or little, and they did not offer me even a plateful, either our own people or others : however, I took patience, having always good courage, waiting for the pea harvest, and some grain from the clearing of the widow Herbert and her son-in-law, who had sown some six or seven acres, not being able to apply elsewhere ; and I can say with truth, that I have assisted every one as much as is possible, but they were little grateful." The Jesuits and Recollets had tolerable supplies on hand, and ground cleared and sown besides ; and they *promised* to assist him with any supplies they might have, " but there were but few liberalities ' made.'"

At this critical time an Indian brought intelligence

of the return of the English squadron. " When this news arrived," writes Champlain, " I was alone in the fort, part of my companions having gone fishing, others to seek for roots, and my servant and the two little ' sauvagesses' (the Indian girls before mentioned) had gone also. About ten o'clock some returned to the settlement, my servant bringing four little bags of roots : he told me that he had seen the English ships about a league from Quebec, behind Cape Levy." Champlain thereupon called a council, and, considering that they were without provisions, powder, match, or prospect of succour, and thus quite unable to hold out, it was resolved that they would endeavour to make the best terms they could, and see what the English would say; but determined, if they would not grant good conditions, to make them feel on landing " what it was to take away all hope."

Shortly after, the English sent a boat with a flag of truce, and a gentleman bearing a letter from the two brothers of the " General Quer" or Guer (sometimes the name is also spelt " Kertk"), who remained at Tadoussac with his ships,—one, named Louis, was to command the fort; the other, Thomas, was " vice-admiral" to his brother. The missive was as follows:

" Monsieur,—In consequence of what our brother told you last year, that sooner or later he would have Quebec, if not succoured, he has charged us to assure you of his friendship as we do of ours; and knowing very well the extreme need of every thing in which you are, desires that you should surrender the fort and settlement to us; assuring you of every

m

kind of courtesy for you and yours, and also of honourable and reasonable terms, such as you may wish. Waiting your reply, we remain, Monsieur, your very affectionate servants,

" Louis and Thomas Guer.

" On board the Filbot, this 19th July, 1629."

To this courteous letter, Champlain replied, that it was true that negligence or risks of the sea had prevented the expected aid from arriving, and, consequently, deprived him of the power of opposing their intentions; that, on the morrow, he would let them know the terms on which he would give up the settlement, and begging them in the meantime to withdraw out of cannon-shot and not to attempt a landing. In the evening, Captain Louis Guer sent for the terms, which were:

" That Guer (Kerk) should show his commission from the king of England, to prove that there really was ' legitimate war' between England and France; also the powers of his brother, commanding the fleet, to treat.

" That a vessel should be given for passage to France, for Champlain and all his companions, with all who had been made prisoners; also all the missionaries, both Jesuits and Recollets, and the two ' sauvagesses,' who had been given to Champlain two years before (what became of the third girl is not stated).

" That all, the ' religious' and others, should be allowed to leave with arms and baggage and all their furniture, and that a sufficient supply of provisions for the passage to France should be given, in exchange for peltry, etc.

" That all should have the most favourable treatment possible, without violence to any.

" That the ship in which they were to embark for France, should be ready in three days after their arrival at Tadoussac, and a vessel provided for the transport of their goods, etc., to that place."

Soon after the reception of these conditions, the English captains sent their ultimatum, which was :

" That Kerk's commission should be shewn, and his powers to his brothers to treat. As to providing a vessel to take Champlain and his people direct to France, that could not be done; but they would give them passage to England and from thence to France, whereby they would avoid being again taken by any English cruiser on their route. For the ' sauvagesses'—that clause could not be granted, for reasons which would be explained. As to leaving with arms and baggage,—the officers might take with them their arms, clothes, and peltries belonging to them, and the soldiers their clothes and a beaver robe each. As for the holy fathers, they must be contented with their robes and books."

All these articles accepted, were duly ratified by David " Kertk" (so spelt this time) at Tadoussac on the 19th August, 1629 (new style).

On the following day the three English vessels cast anchor before Quebec, namely, the " Flibot," of one hundred tons, and ten guns, and two " pataches" (advice boats) of forty tons and six guns each, with about a hundred and fifty men.

Champlain was very desirous to know why he would not be permitted to take with him the two little Indian girls, whom he had taken care of for two years past, " having had them taught needle-work of various kinds and other useful things"; so he went to Captain Louis Kerk, and so persuaded him that he consented to their going, " at which the said girls were very much rejoiced."

Then Captain Louis landed with a hundred and fifty men to take possession of the settlement; the keys of the magazine of the company being delivered to him—not by Du Pont Gravé, but by deputy—the poor man being, as usual, confined to his bed with the gout, and quite unable to act. Kerk gave the keys to a certain Baillif, a Frenchman and native of Amiens, whom he had taken as clerk, and who, with three other Frenchmen, as great rascals as himself, had joined the English voluntarily, " to serve them, and aid them to ruin us," says Champlain, indig-nantly. He then took possession of the fort, treat-ing Champlain with every possible courtesy, but not allowing him to leave Quebec. He permitted mass to be said at Champlain's request, and, " with all kind of affection," gave him a certificate of all sup-plies and property that were found in the fort and settlement, from which it appeared that all the am-munition remaining consisted of forty pounds of powder and fifty-one iron cannon balls.

Kerk took also many articles belonging to the reverend fathers, the Jesuits and Recollets, of which he would not give any account, saying, " If they be given back, (which I do not think they will be,) nothing will be lost, so it is not worth while to mention them; and as for the provisions we have found, we will not spoil paper and ink about them, preferring rather to assist you with ours;" for which Champlain heartily thanked him, "unless he should make him pay very dear for them."

The next day the English flag was hoisted on the fort, the drums beat, the cannon and musketry of the shipping and town fired in token of rejoicing, and solemn possession taken of Quebec in the name of the king of England.

The English conducted themselves with all honour, forbearance, and honesty; not so the French renegades who had joined them, who seemed to have lost no time in filling their pockets. On the very next night, the before-named Frenchman, Baillif, took from the company's chief clerk one hundred livres in gold and silver, a silver cup, "some silk stockings, and other bagatelles," being moreover vehemently suspected of purloining a silver gilt chalice from the chapel, worth a hundred livres or more. Complaints were made to Louis Kerk, who instituted an inquiry, but without effect. Baillif of course swore that he was innocent; "but," says Champlain, "he was without faith or law, although calling himself a Catholic, as did the three others, but who did not scruple to eat flesh on the Friday and Saturday to please the English, who, on the contrary, blamed them for it. I showed him all the evil and reproaches he would one day feel, which did not trouble him much; every wickedness that he could practise against the French he did. From the English we received every kindness; from this wretch every evil. I leave him for what he is worth, expecting that one day God will chastise him for his impieties and blasphemies."

Since the English had taken possession of Quebec, " the days seemed months " to Champlain, who begged Louis Kerk to allow him to go to Tadoussac, and wait for the sailing of the ships, offering to remain with the "general," his brother, which was kindly granted; so, leaving some of his furniture for Louis Kerk's use, he embarked with the remainder of his property and his two little " sauvagesses," poor gouty Du Pont Gravé remaining with the rest of the people, as did the reverend fathers, the Jesuits, etc.

The widow Hebert and her son-in-law, who, with her deceased husband, were the first settlers in Quebec, and who seem to have been the only really industrious and provident residents in the colony, were greatly afraid that their lands would be seized or ravaged by the English; but, on the contrary, they were well treated, every assistance being afforded them, and assurance given that they might remain in as great security of person, property, and trade as before. " Louis Quer" (Kerk), says Champlain, "was courteous, having something of the French nature in him, and loving the nation. He was the son of a Scotchman who had married at Dieppe; so he desired to oblige the French families, preferring their conversation to that of the English, to whom his humour was repugnant! "

The mass of the colonists, not knowing whether to go or to stay, asked Champlain's advice. He told them that, as the exercise of their religion would no longer be free, or even possible, having no more priests, and as they would be deprived consequently of confession, and those holy sacraments which would give their souls repose for ever, they had better dispose of all their peltry, etc., getting as much money as they could for it, and return to France in the way that the English commander had offered ; " for," he added, " you must care more for the soul than the body, and having money with you in France, you can keep above want." They thanked him for his counsel, which they promised to follow, " hoping, nevertheless, to meet again next year, if it pleased God."

On the 24th of July, the vessel of Thomas Kerk set sail for Tadoussac with Champlain on board. About twenty-five leagues from Quebec, a ship was discovered which, on seeing the English, endeavoured to escape. It turned out to be a vessel of the elder De Caen, commanded by his nephew, Emery, who was endeavouring to get secretly to Quebec, to bring away the peltry and other property claimed by the uncle, and to endeavour to trade with the Indians. Kerk fired a gun to bring the Frenchman to, and was answered with a broadside, which killed one of his men. The enemy still endeavouring to get the advantage of the wind, Kerk determined to board, and thereupon ordered Champlain and his companions to go below. It should appear that Kerk was badly seconded by his men, as they went below also, and he was obliged to drive them to the deck with the flat of his sword. He was in a great strait, as few even then would follow him, when, luckily, Emery De Caen, who seems to have been as much afraid as Kerk's men were, cried out for quarter, which Kerk was very glad to grant. De Caen asked to speak with Champlain, whom Kerk rather unwarrantably warned that, if another shot was fired, he should be put to death; telling him to recommend the French to surrender promptly, as if two English ships, then in sight, should come up before the flag was struck, they would all be killed. To which Champlain replied, " that Kerk could certainly kill him, being in his power, but that he would be for ever dishonoured by so retracting the pledge, which both he and his brother Louis had given for the safety of them all; that he could not command the people of the other ship, or prevent them doing their duty as brave men should do, and for which Kerk should rather praise than blame them." Kerk then desired him to offer good terms, which being done, De Caen and his lieutenant went on board the English ship to make their submission.

They then continued their route to Tadoussac, where they found the " General" David Kerk, who received them very kindly. Champlain also met his brother-in-brother, Boullé, who had been made prisoner, and the arch-traitor and rebel, Jacques Michel, who had guided the English in both their expeditions. He was vice-admiral of the fleet, which consisted of five large ships of four to five hundred tons, and about one hundred and twenty men each. "With the exception of the officers," says Champlain, "they were no great things."

The commander in chief, David Quer, Guer, Kertk, or Kerk (for his name is spelt in all these ways), proceeded up the river to Quebec, to see how matters were going on, while Champlain remained at Tadoussac, "passing the time as well as we could till his return." The "General" came back in ten or twelve days, and at supper a few days after, to Champlain's great amazement and anger, produced a letter which he had received from a certain Marsolet, a deserter from the settlement and an abominable scoundrel, who acted as interpreter to the English, to the effect that a canoe had arrived at Quebec, bringing intelligence of a council having been held by the Indians to deliberate whether Champlain should take the two little girls, whom they had given him, to France; and that the result had been that the girls were not to be allowed to go, and the General was requested to detain them.

"I judged immediately," says Champlain, "that the gallant had invented this cunning story to keep the girls," as one of them, named Espérance, had shortly before told him that Marsolet had solicited her to leave Champlain and go with him, promising all sorts of things if she would consent. Champlain represented to the "General" that the girls had been freely given him by the Indians to be brought up in the Christian faith, and that he loved them as his own daughters. He entreated him to allow them to go with him to France, otherwise " they might, by remaining in the country, fall back into the hands of the devil, from which he had extricated them"; and that Marsolet had invented the tale of the Indian council to gain his ends and ruin the poor girls, as he, Champlain, knew, that at the council which had been held at Trois Rivières, there had been no question whatever either of the girls or of Marsolet, and that two men, whom he could produce, could prove that the Indians were very glad that the girls should remain with him. The " General," however, for some reason or other which he did not mention, was not disposed to let the young " sauvagesses" go, notwithstanding the intervention of his brother Thomas and of Michel, and the bitter weeping of the poor girls themselves, " who could neither eat nor drink for crying," begging him, whom they loved as a father, not to abandon them.

" I did all I could," says Champlain, "to save their poor souls"; so he told the " General" that, supposing Marsolet's story to be true, there was still a way to settle the matter, which was to make the Indians a present, and that he would abandon for that purpose beaver-skins and other property to the value of a thousand livres; but the " General" was deaf to his entreaties. One day, however, when in good humour, he gave some hopes of their deliverance when Marsolet should come to Tadoussac; but the artful rascal, on his arrival, persuaded Kerk that the Indians would not accept any present, and that he had better keep the girls as hostages for the good behaviour of the savages; besides, if he should suffer them to depart, and if anything should happen to them afterwards, the Indians would consider it as his (the General's) fault, and much evil might come of it; whereupon the " General" " stiffened" himself anew, and would not hear of the girls' departure. The poor "sauvagesses" continued to weep and lament, but in vain; nevertheless they kept a high spirit, which manifested itself one day in the presence and greatly to the surprise of the " General" and his officers while at supper, when Espérance roundly reproached Marsolet with his indecency, his villainies and treachery. " You know," she exclaimed, " wretch that you are, that I wished to go to France with Monsieur Champlain, who has brought me up, with every possible kindness, teaching me to pray to God, and many other virtuous things, and that the whole country had consented; but you, instead of having compassion on two poor girls, behave worse than a dog to them; but, remember this, though I am only a girl, I will contrive your death, if possible; and if in future you ever shall dare to approach me, I will plant a knife in your breast, if I should die for it. A dog is better than you: he follows those who have given him existence, but you betray and destroy those among whom you received your being, selling your countrymen for money." Marsolet said that "she had learned her lesson well," and turning to her sister, Charité, sneeringly asked " if she had nothing to say to him." "All that I can tell you," she replied, "my companion has said ; I can only add, that if I held your heart, I would eat it, and with better appetite than the meats on that table !"—" Every body admired the courage and discourse of this girl," says Champlain, " who did not speak at all like a ' sauvagesse.' " Some of my readers may possibly differ with him.

Marsolet was astounded at this speech from a girl of twelve years old ; but for all that, the general's heart remained unmoved ; so the poor young girls were raised to the dignity of hostages, to preserve the peace of the country from attacks or inroads of tribes to which they did not belong, or which might not know or care about them. Champlain consoled them, as he best might, with hopes of the return of the French, giving them such useful presents as he could, and telling them to take courage, be good and virtuous, and continue to say the prayers that he had taught them. At his request also, one of the interpreters, named Coulart, promised to let them stay with his wife, which much relieved Champlain's anxiety ; as for the girls, they gratefully promised to be to Coulart and his wife, as daughters, till he should return.

About this time, the arch-renegade, Jacques Michel, "being suddenly seized with great heaviness," remained thirty-five hours without speaking, and then died, "rendering his soul," writes Champlain; "which, if we may judge from the works and actions that he had committed, even on the previous day swearing in a horrible manner, and dying in the ' pretended' religion, I doubt not, is in hell."

There was more gladness than regret among the English at Michel's death; however, he was buried with all the honours of his rank; but the "mourning" lasted but a very little while; on the contrary, the English were never more happy, particularly on board his own ship, "where," slily insinuates Champlain, "there were certain casks of Spanish wine."

The "General," or Admiral, having furnished the fort and settlement at Quebec with all that was necessary for defence and support, and careened and refitted his ships, set sail for England; and on the 20th November, 1629, anchored at "Plemué" (Plymouth), where they heard that peace had been concluded some months before, which greatly displeased the said "General." On the 27th, the Jesuits, Recollets, and all those who wished to return to France, were disembarked in Dover roads, and Champlain proceeded with the ship to London, where he arrived on the 29th.

On the morrow, he obtained an interview with the French Ambassador, to whom he gave a full account of his proceedings, and of all that had happened, complaining bitterly of his fort and himself having been taken fully two months after peace had been proclaimed; but shewing that his surrender had been solely from want of ammunition and provisions, relating the hardships endured, being obliged to seek for roots in the woods for his people's bare subsistence, etc.; all of which the ambassador laid before the king of England, who "gave him good hope of the restoration of the colony, together with all peltry and other goods which had been seized."

Champlain remained nearly five weeks in London, preparing a report for the king of all that had occurred ; the capitulation with General Kerk, and a map of all the country taken by the English and claimed by the French in virtue of first discovery ; and waiting for news from France, but none arriving, the ambassador allowed him to depart, giving him letters for the Cardinal (Richelieu), with the assurance that the English government had promised to give up the colony, and all property captured. He accordingly left London on the 30th December, for " Larie" (Rye), as being the nearest port to Dieppe, meeting on the road the elder De Caen, on his way to London, in the hope of recovering his peltries and other property.[1] Embarking the next day, he arrived safely at Dieppe.

After a few days repose at Dieppe and Rouen, Champlain proceeded to Paris, where he presented himself to the king, Cardinal Richelieu, and the " associates" of the company, giving a full account of his proceedings, etc.   Letters were despatched from the French government, to London, to demand re-

---

[1] De Caen found means not only to disarm suspicion of his treachery and collusion with Michel, but contrived to obtain a sort of compensation for his exclusion from the company of the " Cent Associés."   On the 1st January, 1633, Cardinal Richelieu gave permission to the Sieur Guillaume De Caen to establish colonies on certain islands in the West Indies, with exclusive privileges for a term of years, " provided the said islands were not already inhabited by Christians, and that none but Roman Catholics should be allowed to settle there."   I cannot find any further mention of De Caen and his enterprises.

stitution of the fort and settlement of Quebec, and the other places captured in Canada, and on the coast of Acadia. Restitution of Quebec was promised by the king of England, but no mention made of Acadia. These promises were renewed from time to time, without any appearance even of performance, so that the company finding that " restitution" seemed as far off as ever, supplicated the king to send six ships of war, in company with four of their vessels, to the St. Lawrence, to resume possession of the colony according to agreement ; and that if the English should not consent to give it up, that they " should be constrained by all just and legal methods," *i.e.*, by force. The company proposed to pay the interest of the sum requisite for the equipment of the royal ships. This petition was granted, and the Chevalier de Rasilly was appointed commander of the fleet; and the vessels were prepared for sailing, when the English government, taking umbrage at this extraordinary armament, remonstrated ; and the French king, fully occupied with his Italian wars, put off all interference till they should be over; so that the armament was countermanded, the voyage abandoned, and matters remained for the present *in statu quo*.

Champlain has not left any relation of his subsequent proceedings. The account of his Voyages in New France, which in fact is his autobiography for twenty-seven eventful years of the most interesting period of his life, terminates in 1629-30. He subsequently added a short notice of the events which occurred in the colony, of which he was justly styled

the father, during the year 1631; and in 1632, he
published the whole narrative, with the addition of a
" Treatise on Navigation and of the Duties of a good
Mariner,"[1] and an abridgement of the Christian
doctrine in the French and Huron languages. He
appears to have been fully occupied during his stay
in France, from the end of 1629 to 1632, with the
preparation and publication of his voyages and discoveries, and with pleading the cause of his favourite colony, his own creation, which was in danger of
being abandoned, some considering it as not worth
preserving, having cost large sums, without having
returned any adequate profit. However, he gained
his point, and Canada was restored to France by the
treaty of St. Germain in 1632.

In 1633 the " Company of New France " resumed
all its rights; and Champlain was again named Governor of the Colony of Quebec and all its depend-
encies, where affairs had gone on but badly during
the English occupation, and his absence. The worthy
Father François Du Creux, or " Creuxius," of the
Society of Jesus, thus notices Champlain's arrival at
Quebec: " To the incredible delight both of the
French and natives, Champlain returned. On the
11th of June, at sunrise, a great explosion of bom-
bards was heard, which threw the settlement into
great agitation, lest an English ship, whose arrival
at Tadoussac had been announced three days before,
should have turned out to be an enemy or a pirate;
and what if the peace between England and France

———————

[1] " Traité de la Marine et du Devoir d'un bon Marinier."

should be at an end? But persons sent to explore, brought back the news of Champlain's coming; then fear was changed to gratulation: all would now be well, and the proper administration of Canadian affairs would be restored to full activity by Champlain." The "father of the colony" brought with him ample supplies in men, arms, and munitions of all kinds, for the defence and support of the settlement; and, for its spiritual comfort, a reinforcement of Jesuits. He continued to govern the colony with his usual wisdom and goodness, endeavouring by all means in his power to promote Christianity among the Indians, and he succeeded in establishing a mission with the Hurons. Under his firm and equitable rule, the colony rapidly increased in numbers, wealth, and consequent importance; and at the time of his death some progress was made in the foundation of a college at Quebec.

Towards the end of the year 1635 Champlain died, after an illness of two months and a half, exhibiting during his malady the same firmness, piety, and solicitude for the colony, for which he had always been remarkable; " giving," says De Creux, " in the hour of death, such illustrious evidence of virtue and courage that everyone was astonished. His remains were followed to the grave by the whole population with unfeigned grief."

From this notice of his career, it will be seen that Champlain was no ordinary man. Unintimidated by the repeated failures of preceding attempts, he followed up his plans with as much resolution as sagacity. But for him Quebec would probably have never existed. Undeterred by the cabals and intrigues, lay and clerical, constantly going on in France; unmoved by the continual discords and quarrels of rival companies, he steered a straightforward course, avoiding giving umbrage to any, if not satisfying all. Trusting nothing to others that he could do himself, he penetrated, almost alone, to the unexplored countries of distant Indian tribes ; exhibiting rare perseverance, energy, and courage, rebuking cruelty, encouraging the good, and omitting no opportunity of promulgating the truths of Christianity.

Notwithstanding a considerable dose of credulity,[1] he was endowed with rare penetration. His views were just, and no one knew better how to decide in difficulties, or to support them with more patience and constancy; no dangers daunted him, and he never lost sight of his object. His zeal for the interests of his country was ardent and disinterested. With a feeling heart he was always ready to succour the unfortunate, more careful of the welfare of others

---

[1] In 1604 Champlain published a relation of his first voyage to Canada ; in it he mentions a strange and frightful monster called "gougou," giving at the same time the names of his authorities. This story, which, in a great measure, gave rise to the accusation of credulity, was suppressed in the general relation of his voyages in 1632. The "dragon," the two legs of the camelion, and the no-legs of the bird of Paradise, the mode of hatching the same, etc., described in the present manuscript, show that, however he may have got over extreme credulity in later years, in his first voyages he had a strong belief in the marvellous—but that quality belonged in a degree to the age in which he lived.

than of his own. A faithful narrator, an enterprising and active traveller; nothing escaped his attention and observation. He was a good geometrician and able navigator. The war to which he seems to have incited, or in which at least he joined, the Algonquins, Hurons, and other tribes against the Iroquois, can hardly be justified; but the result of his policy, if policy it was, proved favourable, in bringing to and confirming in his alliance the tribes more immediately surrounding the infant colony.

BRIEF NARRATIVE OF THE MOST REMARKABLE THINGS THAT SAMUEL CHAMPLAIN OF BROUAGE, OBSERVED IN THE WESTERN INDIES;

DURING THE VOYAGE WHICH HE MADE TO THE SAME, IN THE YEARS ONE THOUSAND FIVE HUNDRED AND NINETY-NINE TO ONE THOUSAND SIX HUNDRED AND TWO,—AS FOLLOWS.

HAVING been employed in the army of the king, which was in Brittany, under Messieurs the Maréchal d'Aumont de St. Luc,[1] and the Maréchal de Brissac,[2] during some years in the quality of maréchal de logis,[3] until his majesty, in

[1] Maréchal d'Aumont. Jean d'Aumont, born in 1522, of an ancient and noble family, entered the career of arms very early, and distinguished himself by his bravery during the Piedmontese war. Henry III created him Knight of the Saint Esprit in 1578, and Marshal of France in the following year. D'Aumont signalized himself at the battle of Ivry. He was named governor of Poitou by Henry IV, and by his prudent conduct kept that province from rising for the League. The king sent him to Brittany to oppose the Duke de Mercœur. He was killed by a musket-shot at the siege of Camper, on the 19th of August, 1595, aged seventy-three years.

[2] Maréchal de Brissac. Charles, second Duke de Cossé Brissac, peer and marshal of France. He gave up Paris, of which he was governor, to Henry IV, on the 22nd March, 1594. He served in the war in Brittany till its close, and died at Brissac, in Anjou, in 1621.

[3] "Maréchal de logis"—quarter-master.

the year one thousand five hundred and ninety-eight, had
reduced the said country of Brittany to obedience,[1] and dismissed his army; and finding myself by this means without
any charge or employment, I resolved, in order not to remain
idle, to find means of making a voyage to Spain, and, being
there, to acquire and cultivate acquaintance, in order, by
their favour and interposition, to arrange so as to be able to
embark in one of the ships of the fleet, which the king of
Spain sends every year to the western Indies; to the end,
in so embarking, to be able at my return to make a true
report to his majesty (Henry IV) of the particularities
which could not be known to any Frenchman, for the reason
that they have not free access there.

[1] Reduction of Brittany. The greater part of Brittany held out for the
League against the king (Henry IV), under the command of the Duke
de Mercœur, aided by the Spaniards under the Archduke Albert of
Austria.

Philippe Emanuel de Lorraine, Duke de Mercœur, was born at
Nomény, in 1558. Attached to the Duke of Guise, he was about to be
arrested at the States of Blois in 1588, but the queen, Louise de Lorraine, his sister, gave him timely warning, and he escaped. He then
openly embraced the party of the League, withdrew to his government
of Brittany, called in the aid of the Spaniards, and gave them possession
of the port of Blavet in 1591. He made his submission to Henry IV
in April, 1598, and was pardoned at the intercession of Gabrielle
d'Estrées, lately created Duchess of Beaufort, who, however, previously
stipulated that the duke should give his daughter, Françoise, one of the
richest heiresses in France, in marriage to the son of Henry IV, César,
Duke de Vendôme. In 1601 the Emperor Rodolph offered De Mercœur
the command of his army in Hungary against the Turks. He endeavoured with only fifteen thousand men to raise the siege of Chanicha,
which Ibrahim Pacha had invested with sixty thousand. He was forced
to retire, but his retreat passed for one of the most skilful then known.
Obliged in the following year to return to France, he died on the way,
at Nuremberg, in 1602.

In order, then, to accomplish my design, I went to Blavet,[1] where at that time was a garrison of Spaniards, in which place I found an uncle of mine called "the Provençal captain," considered to be one of the good mariners of France, and who, in that year, had been engaged by the king of Spain as Pilot-General of his sea armies.

My said uncle having received the commands of Monsieur le Maréchal de Brissac, to conduct the ships in which the Spaniards of the garrison of Blavet were embarked, in order to repass them to Spain, as it had been promised, I embarked with him, in a great ship of five hundred tons, named the "Saint Julian," which had been taken, and engaged for the said voyage; and having quitted Blavet in the beginning of the month of August, we arrived ten days afterwards near to Cape Finisterre, which we could not perceive on account of a great fog which arose from the sea, in consequence of which all our vessels were separated, and even our vessel-admiral (admirande), of the fleet was nearly lost, having touched upon a rock, and taken in much water, in which ship (and over the whole fleet) the General Soubriago commanded, having been sent by the king of Spain to Blavet for that purpose.

---

[1] Blavet, the last town held by the Spaniards in Brittany, was, together with all the places they possessed in Picardy, given up by the treaty of Vervins, in June 1598, and thus the whole province was submitted to the king's authority.

Blavet, or Port Louis, a fortified town with citadel and harbour in Brittany, department of the Morbihan, at the embouchure of the river Blavet; the town being ruined during the wars of the League, Louis XIII rebuilt it from the former materials, erected a fort, and gave it his name.

On the following day, the weather having cleared up, all our vessels rejoined, and we proceeded to the Isles of Bayona, in Galicia, in order to refit the admiral's ship which was much injured.

Having sojourned six days at these islands, we made sail, and three days after came in sight of Cape St. Vincent; having doubled the said cape, we proceeded to the port of Callix (Cadiz), which, having entered, the soldiers were disembarked; and after the landing, the French ships that had been engaged for the voyage, were dismissed, and sent back, each one to its port, excepting the said ship, the St. Julian, which, having been observed by the General Soubriago to be a strong vessel, and a good sailer, was engaged by him for the service of the king of Spain: and thus the "Provençal captain," my uncle, remained still in it; and we sojourned at the port of Callix an entire month, during which I had the opportunity of examining that city.

Departing from the said Callix, we continued to St. Lucar de Barameda, which is at the entry of the river of Seville, where we remained three months, during which time I went to Seville, and took drawings of it, and of the other (St. Lucar de Barameda), which I have judged fitting to represent in the best manner that I could in the following.

During the three months that we remained at St. Lucar de Barameda, there arrived a patache,[1] coming from Porto-rico, to inform the king of Spain that the army of England was at sea, with the design of taking the said Porto-rico: upon which advice, the said king of Spain, in order to

[1] " Patache"—advice-boat.

las norcades

Marais salans.

estang

bois deltuiers

ternant e

S rariois

forons de pains

St Loucque de batame de

Rofes

nostre signore de Rege

Cotar

Cette dicte echelle contient 2m<e>lieux et demye

succour it, had an armament prepared, of the number of twenty ships, and of two thousand men, soldiers, and mariners; among which ships, that named the St. Julian was retained, and my uncle was commanded to make the voyage in it, by which I received extreme joy, promising myself by this means to satisfy my desire: and for that purpose I readily resolved to go with him; but whatever diligence could be made to repair, victual, and equip the said ships, to enable them to put to sea, when at the point of departure, there arrived news by another patache, that it had been taken by the English; in consequence of which, the said voyage was broken off, to my great regret, to find myself thus frustrated in my hope.

Now, at the same time, the armament of the king of Spain, which was accustomed to go every year to the Indies, was getting ready at the said St. Lucar, where there arrived, by command of the king, a noble named Don Francisque Colombe, a knight of Malta, to be general of the said armament, who, seeing our vessel prepared and ready for service, and knowing, by the report which had been made to him, that it was strong and very good under sail for its burthen, resolved to make use of it, and take it at the ordinary freight, which is one crown per ton per month; so that I had occasion to rejoice seeing my hopes revive, and the more so that the Provençal captain, my uncle, having been retained by General Soubriago to serve elsewhere, and thus not able to make the voyage, committed to me the charge of the said ship, to have the care of it, which I accepted very willingly: and upon that we sought the said Seigneur, General

Colombe, to know if he would have it for agreeable that I should make the voyage, which he freely granted, with evidence of being well pleased, promising me his favour and assistance, which he has not since denied me upon occasion.

The said armament set sail in the beginning of the month of January, in the year 1599, and the wind blowing always very fresh, in six days after we arrived in sight of the Canary Isles.

Leaving the said Canary Islands, we passed by the Gulf of Las Damas, having the wind astern, so that in two months and six days after our departure from St. Lucar, we got sight of an island named La Deseade, which is the first island that pilots must necessarily recognise in going to all the other islands and ports of the Indies.

This island is round and tolerably high from the sea, and is seven leagues in circumference, full of wood and uninhabited, but there is good anchorage on the eastern side.

From the said isle we passed to another island, called Guadaloupe, which is very mountainous and inhabited by savages;[1] in it there are numbers of good ports, in one of which, named Macou, we took in water, and as we landed we saw more than three hundred savages, who fled into the mountains at our approach, without it being in our power to overtake them, any one of them being more quick in running than any of our men who tried to follow them; seeing which, we returned to our ships after having taken

[1] Guadaloupe. The first settlement in Guadaloupe was established by the French in 1635, by Messrs. Du Plissis and Olive.

cette dicte Isle est a

GARDA
LOVPPE

E

ISLAND

15 de grez

pet denacou

Lieux

1   2   3   4   5   6   7

OF GUADALOUPE.

PEARL FISHERY.

in some water and refreshments, such as cabbages and fruits of pleasant taste.

This island is about twenty leagues in length and twelve in breadth, and its form is shown in the following figure.

After having remained two days in the aforesaid port of Macou, on the third we again put to sea, and passed between islands called Las Virgines, which are in such quantity, that their number cannot be told for certain; but although there are more than eight hundred discovered, they are all desert and uninhabited; the land very high and full of wood, both of palms and ramasques,[1] which are common, like oaks or elms. There are a number of good ports and havens in the said isles.

From these isles we sailed to the island of La Marguerite, where pearls are fished. In this island there is a good town, which is called by the same name, La Marguerite. The isle is very fertile in corn and fruits; every day more than three hundred canoes leave the harbour of the said town, which go about a league to sea to fish for pearls, in ten or twelve fathoms water. The said fishing is done by negroes, slaves of the king of Spain, who take a little basket under their arm, and with it plunge to the bottom of the sea, and fill it with ostrormes, which resemble oysters; then go up again into their canoes, and return to the port to discharge them, in a spot destined for that purpose, when the officers of the king of Spain receive them.

From this island we went to St. Juan de Porto-rico, which we found very desolate; both the town, as well as the castle or fortress, which is very strong; and the port

___

[1] "Ramasques"—wide-spreading, branching, and bushy trees.

also is very good, and sheltered from all winds, saving the north-east, which blows strait into the harbour.

The town is very mercantile ; it had been, shortly before, pillaged by the English, who had left marks of their visit ; most of the houses had been burnt, and there were not four persons to be found there, except some negroes, who told us that the merchants of the place had been for the greater part carried off prisoners by the English, and the others, who had been able to escape, had fled into the mountains, from whence they had not yet dared to come back, on account of the apprehension they had of the return of the English, who had loaded all the twelve ships, of which their armament was composed, with sugar, hides, gold, and silver : for we found still in the town quantities of sugar, hides, canifiste,[1] honey of cane,[2] and preserves of ginger, which the English could not take away.   They carried off also fifty pieces of artillery of cast iron, which they took in the fortress, into which we went, and found all ruined, and the ramparts thrown down. There were some Indians who had retired there, and had begun to reconstruct the ramparts ; the General inquired of them, how the place had been taken in so short a time ? One of them, who spoke tolerably good Spanish, said, that neither the governor of the castle, nor the oldest men of the country thought that within two leagues there was any place of landing, according to the report which had been made by the pilots of the place, who had even assured them, that for

---

[1] Canifiste, from "Caneficier," the name given in the Antilles to the cassia tree.   Cassia fistula (Linn.)—the keleti of the Caribs, producing the cassia Nigra of commerce.

[2] Honey of canes—molasses ?

more than six leagues from the said castle, there was no spot where an enemy could make a descent, which was the cause that the governor kept less on his guard, and in which he was much deceived, for at half a league from the castle, on the eastern side, there was a place where the English landed very conveniently, leaving their ships, which were of the burthen of two hundred, one hundred and fifty, and one hundred tons, in the offing, near the said spot, and took their time so well, that they arrived at night in the roads without being perceived, no one apprehending such a thing. They landed six hundred men, with the design of pillaging the town only, not thinking of making any greater effect, considering the castle to be stronger and better guarded. They brought with them three culverins, to batter the defences of the town, and found themselves at the point of daylight at the distance of a musket shot from it, to the great astonishment of the inhabitants.

The said English placed two hundred men at the passage of a little river, which is between the town and the castle, to prevent (as they did) the soldiers of the guard of the castle, who were lodged in the town, as well as the inhabitants who might endeavour to escape, from entering the fortress; and the other four hundred men attacked the town, where they found no resistance, so that in less than two hours they were masters of it; and having learned that there were no soldiers in the castle, nor any supply of provisions, on account of the governor having, by order of the king of Spain, sent all that had been there to Cartagena, where they thought that the enemy would make a descent, hoping

to receive other supplies from Spain, being the nearest port
to which their vessels came.

The English summoned the governor, and offered him
good terms if he would surrender; if not, that they would
make him suffer all the rigor of war; fearing which, the
said governor surrendered, on condition that his life should
be safe, and embarked with the English, not daring to return to Spain. It was only fifteen days since the English
had departed from the town, where they had remained a
month.

After their departure, the aforesaid Indians had returned,
and endeavoured to repair the fortress, expecting the army
of our general, who caused a report to be made of the recital
of those Indians, which he sent to the king of Spain, and
commanded the Indian who had first spoken, to go and seek
those who had fled into the mountains, who, on his word,
returned to their houses, receiving such contentment at seeing the general and being delivered from the English, that
they forgot their past losses.

The said Island of Porto-rico is pretty agreeable, although
it is a little mountainous, as the following figure shows.[1]—
It is filled with quantities of fine trees, such as cedars, palms,
firs, palmettoes, and another kind of tree which is called

[1] The town of Porto-rico was founded in 1510. It was attacked by
Drake and Hawkins in 1595, but the Spaniards, being apprised of their
coming, had made such preparations, that Drake was forced to retire,
after burning the Spanish ships that were in the harbour. In 1598 an
expedition was fitted out by George Clifford, Earl of Cumberland, to
conquer the island. He disembarked his men secretly and attacked the
town, when, according to the Spanish accounts, he met with vigorous
resistance from the inhabitants (Champlain's account from eyewitnesses

ceste dictte Isle es

Bocas de
Inferni
S. Ic

P. dgo

pt Torico

E

5

ISLAND OF F

st a 48 degrez

G ROSSO

e los
nos

OVAN DE PORTE Ricor Guadianitta

pot de la guade

10   15

Thieux

PORTO RICO.

sombrade,[1] from which, as it grows, the tops of its branches, falling to the earth, take root immediately, and produce other branches which fall and take root in the same way. And I have seen these trees of such extent that they covered more than a league and a quarter. It bears no fruit, but is very agreeable, having a leaf like that of a laurel and a little more tender.

There are also, in the said island, quantities of good fruits, such as plantes,[2] oranges, lemons of strange size,[3] ground gourds, which are very good, algarobes,[4] pappittes,[5] and a fruit named coraçon,[6] because it is in the form of a heart, of

and sufferers is very different) ; but in a few days the garrison of four hundred men surrendered, and the whole island submitted to the Eng- lish. The possession of the island being deemed of great importance, the Earl adopted the harsh measure of exiling the inhabitants to Carta- gena, and in spite of the protests and remonstrances of the unfortunate Spaniards, the plan was put in execution; a few only escaped. How- ever the English soon found it impossible to keep the island ; a grievous malady carried off three-fourths of the troops. Cumberland, deceived in his hopes, returned to England, leaving the command to Sir John Berkeley. The mortality spreading daily more and more, forced the English to evacuate the island, and the Spaniards soon after resumed possession of their dwellings.

Champlain's account of the state of the island after the departure of the English, and of the cowardice of the governor, is curious ; there is, however, some confusion in his dates, and as to the time that the Eng- lish occupation lasted.

[1] Sombrade—from " sombra," Span.—leafy shade. " Ficus americana maxima," the " Clusea rosea" of St. Domingo, or " Figuier maudit mar- ron."

[2] Plantes—" Plantano" of the Spaniards, a species of banana, called in the Canaries " plantano."

[3] Lemons of strange size—Shaddock ?

[4] Algarobe. See forward, page 25.

[5] Pappette—" Curica papaia" (Linn.)—papaw-tree.

[6] Coraçon. Anona Muricata, or Corassol, from the Spanish "Corazon,"

the size of the fist, and of a yellow and red colour; the skin very delicate, and when it is pressed, it gives out an odoriferous humour; and that which is good in this fruit is like thick milk, and has a taste like sugared cream.

There are many other fruits which are not much esteemed, although they are good; there is also a root called "cassave"[1] which the Indians eat instead of bread.

There grows neither corn nor wine in all this island. In it there are a great quantity of cameleons which, it is said, live on air; this I cannot assure although I have seen them many times. It has the head rather pointed, the body somewhat long for its size, that is to say, of one foot and a half, and has only two legs, which are in front; the tail very pointed, the colours mingled grey and yellowish. The said cameleon is here represented.[2]

The best merchandise in the island is sugar, ginger, canifiste, honey of canes, tobacco, quantity of hides of oxen, cows, and sheep. The air is very hot, and there are little birds which resemble parrots, called perriquitos, of the size of a sparrow, with a round tail, and which are taught to speak: there are a great number in that isle.

The said island is about seventy leagues in length and forty in breadth, surrounded by good ports and havens, and lies east and west.

We remained at Porto-rico about a month; the general

—heart, so called from the shape of the fruit. Some writers derived the name from Curaçoa, supposing the seed to have been brought by the Dutch from that island. The native name was " memin."

[1] Cassava—Jatropha Manihot.   [2] See frontispiece.

left about three hundred soldiers, as garrison in the fortress, and caused forty-six pieces of brass cannon, which had been at Blavet, to be placed there.

On leaving Porto-rico our general divided our galleons into three squadrons. He retained four with him, and sent three to Porto-bello, and three to New Spain, of which number was the vessel in which I was; and each galleon had its patache. The said general went to Terra-Firma, and we coasted all the Island of St. Domingo on the north side, and went to a port of the said island, named Porto Platte, to inquire if there were any strange vessels on the coast, because no foreigners are permitted to traffic there, and those who do go there, run the risk of being hung or sent to the galleys, and their ships confiscated; and to keep them in greater fear of approaching the land, the king of Spain gives freedom to any negroes who may discover a foreign vessel and give notice to the general of the army, or to the governor; and there are negroes who would go a hundred and fifty leagues on foot, night and day, to give such notice and acquire their liberty.

We landed at Porto Platte, and went about a league inland without meeting any one, excepting a negro who was preparing to go and give notice, but meeting with us, he went no farther, and informed our "admiral" that there were two French ships at the port of Mancenilla; where the said admiral resolved to go, and for that purpose we left the said Porto Platte, which is a good port sheltered from all winds, and where there are three, four, and five fathoms water.

3

From the above Porto Platte we proceeded to the port of Mancenilla, at which port we learned that the aforesaid two vessels were at the port of Mosquittes, near La Tortue, which is a little island thus named, opposite the entrance of the said port, where, arriving the next day about three o'clock in the afternoon, we perceived the above two ships, which were putting to sea to avoid us, but too late; seeing which, and that there were no means of escape, the crew of one of the vessels, which was fully a league at sea, abandoned their ship, and having thrown themselves into their boat, escaped to land. The other ship ran aground and broke to pieces, at the same time the crew escaped to land like the other, and there only remained one mariner in it, who, being lame and somewhat ill, could not fly. He told us that the vessels which were lost were from Dieppe.

There is a very good entrance to the port of Mosquittes, of more than two thousand paces in width, and there is a hidden sand-bank, so that it is necessary to keep near to the land on the east side in entering the said port, in which there is good anchorage; there is an island inside where there is shelter from the north wind, which strikes directly into the harbour. This place is tolerably pleasant from the number of trees which grow there; the land is rather high; but there are such quantities of small flies, like chesans, or gnats, which sting in so strange a fashion, that if a man were to go to sleep and should be stung in the face, puffy swellings of a red colour, enough to disfigure him, would rise from the sting.

Having learned from the lame mariner who was taken in

the French vessel, that there were thirteen great ships, French, English, and Flemish, half armed for war, half with merchandise, our admiral resolved to go and take them at the port of St. Nicolas where they were, and for that purpose prepared three galleons of the burthen of five hundred tons each, and four pataches. We proceeded in the evening to cast anchor in a bay called Monte Christo, which is very good and sheltered from the south-east and from the west, and is remarkable for a mountain which is straight above the harbour, so high that it can be discerned from fifteen leagues at sea. The said mountain is very white and shining in the sun.

For two leagues round the said harbour the land is rather low, covered with a quantity of wood, and there is a very good fishery, and a good port under the mountain.

The following morning we proceeded to Cape St. Nicolas to seek the aforesaid ships, and about three o'clock arrived in the bay of the said Cape, and cast anchor as near as it was possible, the wind being adverse to our entering.

Having anchored, we perceived the vessels of the above mentioned merchants, at which our admiral rejoiced greatly, being assured of taking them. All the night we did all that was possible to endeavour to enter the harbour, and when morning came, the admiral took counsel of the captains and pilots as to what was to be done. They told him that the worst they had to think of was what the enemies might do to escape; that it was impossible for them to fly, saving under favour of the night, having the wind fair; that, in fact they would not hazard it in the day-time, seeing their seven armed ships; also that if they wished to make resistance, they would place their vessels at the entrance of the harbour, anchored stem and stern, with all their guns on one side, and their tops well fenced with cables and hides, and that if they saw that they were getting the worst, they would abandon their ships, and throw themselves on land. To prevent this, the admiral should advance his ships as near to the harbour as possible, batter the enemies with his cannon, and land one hundred of his best soldiers to prevent their so escaping. This plan was resolved on, but the enemies did not do as it had been expected; for they made their preparations during the night, and when the morning came they set sail and came straight towards our ships, by which they must of necessity pass, in order to get the wind of us. This resolution changed the courage of the Spaniards, and softened their rhodomontades. It was then for us to lift anchor, and with such promptitude, that in the admiral's ship they cut the cable at the hawse-hole, not having time to raise the anchor. So we also set sail, giving and receiving cannonades. At last they gained the wind on us, and we pursued them all day and the following night until the morning, when we saw them four leagues from us, which our admiral perceiving, he abandoned the pursuit to continue our route; but it is very certain that if he had wished he could have taken them, having better ships, more men and munitions of war. The foreign vessels were only preserved by default of courage of the Spaniards.

During this chase, there happened a laughable thing which deserves to be related. A patache of four or five

Le port Payag[.]

A HARBOUR IN

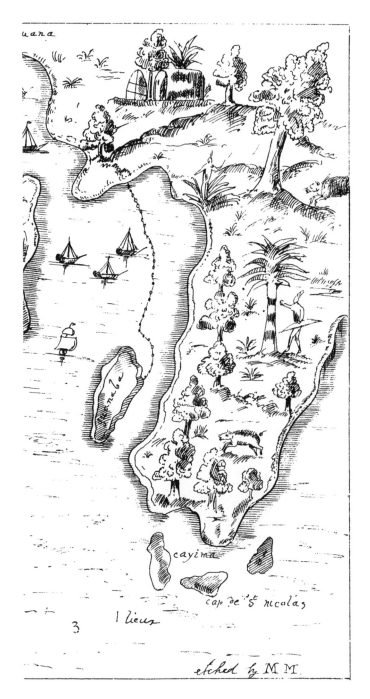

uana.

meba

cayima

cap de St nicolas

3   1 lieus

etched by M M.

St DOMINGO.

tons was seen mingled with our ships. It was hailed frequently, as to whence it came, with orders to lower the sails, but there was no reply : and although some guns were fired at it, it continued to go before the wind, which moved our admiral to have it chased by two of our pataches, which, in less than two hours, overtook and approached it, calling out always for the sails to be lowered, without any answer ; nor would the soldiers board it ; although no one was seen at the helm, so that the commander of the pataches said that it was steered by a devil, and forced the soldiers, as many as twenty, by menaces, to go on board, who found nothing ; they only brought away the sails, and left the hull to the mercy of the sea.

A report being made of this to the admiral, and of the fright that the soldiers had shewn, it gave matter for laughter to all.

Leaving the island of St. Domingo, we continued our route to New Spain.

The aforesaid island of St. Domingo is large, being one hundred and fifty leagues long, and sixty broad, very fertile in fruits, cattle, and good merchandise, such as sugar, canifiste, ginger, honey of canes, cotton, hides of oxen, and some furs. There are numerous good ports, and good anchorage, and only one town, named L'Espaignolle,[1] inhabited by Spaniards ; the rest of the population is Indian, good-natured people, and who much like the French nation, with whom they traffic as often as they can, but this is without the knowledge of the Spaniards. It is also the place where

[1] Now San Domingo.

the French trade the most in those quarters, and where they have most access, although with little freedom.

This country is rather hot, and particularly mountainous; there are no mines of gold or silver, but only of copper.

Leaving, then, this island, we coasted along the island of Cuba, on the south side, the land rather high, and proceeded to reconnoitre some small islands, which are called the Caymans, to the number of six or seven. In three of them there are three good harbours, but it is a dangerous passage, on account of the shallows and banks which are there, and it is not good to adventure in it unless the route is well known.

We anchored between the islands, and remained one day; I landed on two of them, and found a very fine and agreeable harbour. I walked about a league inland, through very thick woods, and caught some rabbits, which are in great quantities, some birds, and a lizard as large as my thigh, of a grey and dead-leaf[1] colour. The island is very flat and level, and all the others the same; we also landed on another, which was not so agreeable; but we brought away some very good fruits, and there were such quantities of birds, that at our landing there rose so great a number, that for more than two hours after the air was filled with them: and there were others, which could not fly, so that we took them pretty easily; these are of the size of a goose, the head very large, the beak very wide, low on their legs, the feet like those of a water hen. When these birds are plucked, there is not more flesh on them than on a dove, and

---

[1] Feuille-morte, whence "phillemoti," brownish.

it has a very bad taste. We raised the anchor the same day, towards evening, with a very fair wind, and the next day, about three o'clock in the afternoon, we arrived at a place called "La Sonde,"[1] a very dangerous place, as for more than five leagues there are only shallows, with the exception of . . .[2] leagues in length, and three in width; when we were in the middle of the said channel, we lay to, and the sailors cast out their lines to catch fish, of which they took so large a quantity, that they could not find room enough for them on board the ships. This fish is of the size of a dorade,[3] of a red colour, and very good if eaten fresh, for it will not keep, or salt, but becomes putrid shortly. The lead must be always in hand in passing through this channel; on leaving which, one of our pataches was lost at sea, without our knowing the cause; the soldiers and mariners saved themselves by swimming, some on planks, others on oars, others as they best could, and returned from more than two . . .[4] to our ship, which they met with very *à propos,* and we picked them up in our boats which were sent out for them.

[1] A difficult channel, called by the Spaniards the "Sound of Mexico," abounding in fish, especially Dorades.
"We pursued our route till we arrived at a place which the Spaniards call the Sound of Mexico, for in that place we often cast the sound... During this time we took great diversion in fishing, particularly dorades, on which we made great cheer."—Gage's *Voyage to Mexico in* 1625, from French translation by the Sieur de Beaulieu, Hües O'Neil : 2 vols., Paris, 1676.
[2] Hiatus in MS.
[3] Sparus aurata (Linn.), Brame de Mer—the Bahama dorade is called "porgy."
[4] Hiatus in MS.

Eight days afterwards, we arrived at St. Jean de Luz,[1] which is the first port of New Spain, where the galleons of the king of Spain go every year to be laden with gold, silver, precious stones, and cochineal, to take to Spain.

The said port of St. Jean de Luz is fully four hundred leagues from Porto-rico. On the island, there is a very good fortress, as well by its situation, as by its good ramparts, well furnished with all that is necessary; and there are two hundred soldiers in the garrison, which are enough for the place. This fortress comprises all the island, which is six hundred paces long, and two hundred and fifty paces wide; besides which fortress there are houses built on piles in the water; and for more than six leagues at sea, there are only shallows, which cause that ships cannot enter this

---

[1] The fort or castle of San Juan d'Ulloa is evidently meant, but whether it bore that name when Champlain was there, or whether he confounded the St. Jean de Luz of Spain with San Juan d'Ulloa, is a moot point. In Mercator and Hondius's maps, Amsterdam, 10th edition, 1628, St. Juan d'*Uloa* (Ulloa) is placed on the twenty-sixth degree of north latitude, at the mouth of the river " Lama" (Rio del Norte). The town of Villa Rica, is laid down in the actual position of Vera Cruz, but no mention of either St. Juan de Luz, or d'Ulloa; and in Gage's *Voyage with the Spanish Fleet to the West Indies and Mexico*, 1625, it is styled Sñ Juan d'Ulhua, otherwise Vera Cruz.

" The proper name of the town is Sñ Juan d'Ulhua, otherwise Vera Cruz, from the old harbour of Vera Cruz, which is six leagues from it. But the harbour of the old Vera Cruz being found too dangerous for ships, on account of the violence of the north wind, it was entirely abandoned by the Spaniards, who went to St. Juan d'Ulhua, where their vessels found a safe anchorage by means of a rock which serves as a strong defence against the winds; and in order to perpetuate the memory of this happy adventure, chancing on a Good Friday, to the name of St. Juan d'Ulhua they added that of the True Cross, taken from the first harbour, which was discovered on the Holy Friday of the year 1519."—Gage's *Voyage to Mexico*, etc., 1625.

port, if they do not well know the entrance of the channel, for which entrance you must steer to the south-west; but it is certainly the most dangerous port that can be found, and there is no shelter, excepting on the north side of the fortress; in the walls of the fort are numerous rings of bronze, where the vessels are moored, which are sometimes so crowded together, that when it blows from the north, which is very dangerous, the said vessels are much crushed, although they are moored fore and aft.[1]

The said port is only two hundred paces in width, and two hundred and fifty in length. The place is only kept for the convenience of the galleons which come, as it has been said, from Spain, to load with the merchandise, and gold and silver, which are drawn from New Spain.

On the other side of the castle, and about two thousand paces from it, on terra firma, there is a small, but very trading town, called Bouteron. At four leagues from the said Bouteron, there is also another town, named Vera-Crux, which is in a very fine situation, and two leagues from the sea.

Fifteen days after our arrival at the said St. Jean de Luz, I went, with the permission of our admiral, to " Mechique "

---

[1] " The boats towed our ships, one after the other, through the midst of the sunken rocks, which makes this port one of the most dangerous that I have seen in all my voyages in the north or south seas...We cast our anchors in the haven, but as they were not sufficient to assure our vessels in so dangerous a port, we added the assistance of many cables, which were fastened to great rings of iron, fixed expressly in the walls of the castle to guarantee ships thereby from the violence of the north wind."—Gage's *Voyage.*

(Mexico), distant from that place one hundred leagues, always going inland.

It is impossible to see or desire a more beautiful country than this kingdom of New Spain, which is three hundred leagues in length, and two hundred in breadth.

Making this journey to "Mechique," I admired the fine forests, filled with the most beautiful trees that one could wish to see, such as palms, cedars, laurel, orange, and lemon trees. Palmistes, gouiave, accoiates,[1] good Bresil,[2] and

---

[1] See forward, pages 28 and 29.

[2] Brazil, or Brésil wood—Cæsalpinia. Two species of Brazil wood are used in dyeing, Cæs. Echinata (Lamarck), and Cæs. Sappan (Linn.) The first is the Brazil wood, or Brésillet, of Pernambuco, a large tree growing naturally in South America, used in commerce for red dye. The second is indigenous in India, where it is used for the same purpose, and known in the trade as sappan wood ; in France, " Brésellet des Indes."

The origin of the name " Brazil," or " Brésil," for this wood, was long a moot point, whether the country took its name from the tree, or the tree from the country. Many early writers (and some modern) have thought that it was derived from the country. The Sieur de Rochefort, in his *Histoire Naturelle et Morale des Antilles d'Amérique"* (Rotterdam, 1658), says : " Le bois de Brésil est ainsi nommé à cause que le premier qui a esté veu en Europe, avoit esté apporté de la Province du Brésil, où il croist en plus grande abondance qu'en aucun endroit de l'Amérique"; and Savary, in his *Dictionnaire du Commerce*, writes : " C'est un bois dont on se sert pour teindre en rouge, et qui est ainsi nommé puisqu'il est d'abord venu du Brésil, province de l'Amérique." I could cite more modern authorities, written and oral, for within the last month I heard the derivation of the country asserted by a gentleman of no slight pretensions to learning.

Unfortunately for the above theory, the names " Brésil" and " Brésillet" are mentioned in an " ordonnance" of John, king of France, dated London, 16th September, 1358. " Nous avons entendu plusieurs marchants, Lombards et autres, qui ont trait, ou faict traire hors du dict Royaume,—guerdes, garances, ' *Brésils*, et autres teintures.' "

Again, in the *Règlements pour le Mestier de Draperie de la Ville de*

Campesche wood, which are all trees common to the country, with an infinity of other kinds, that I cannot recite on account of their diversity, and which give such contentment to the sight, with the quantities of birds of divers plumage,

Troyes, 360 : " Nous avons ordené, et ordenons que dores-en-avant, aucune teintures ne puisse ou doie taindre draps au laines en ycelle Ville de Troies, mais que de garde, de garance, de *Brésil*, et d'autres meilleures taintures," etc.

Also in the *Statuts et Règlements pour les Drapiers de la Ville de Rouen*, 4th December and 5th January, 1378, *Brésil* is mentioned, and it is to be found in *Ordonnances* of the years 1368, 1398, and 1400. In the very ancient MS. statutes of the town of Abbeville, *Brésil* is named : " Que à Selle neuve, ne sait mis en œuvre basenne *Bresillé*." Finally, Muratori, in his *Antiq. Ital. Med. Ævi*, vol. ii, cites a charter of the year 1193, in which " Brazil" appears. " Scilicet de omnibus drappis de batilicio, de lume zucarina, de *Brasile*," etc.

The antiquity of the name is thus clearly shown, the origin is most probably " brasa," red, flame-colour, incandescent.

We have the quaint authority of Barros as to the origin of the name of the country, Brazil. " This country had at first the name of Santa Croce, Holy Cross, on account of that which was raised there ; but the demon, who loses by this standard of the cross the empire which he had over us, and which had been taken from him by the mediation of the merits of Jesus Christ, destroyed the cross, and caused the country to be called Brazil, the name of a red wood. This name has entered into the mouth of every one, and that of Holy Cross is lost, as if it was more important that a name should come from a wood used to dye clothes, rather than from that wood which gives virtue to all the sacraments—means of our salvation—because it was dyed with the blood of Jesus Christ spilled upon it."

Thus it is evident that the name Brazils was given to the country by the Portuguese, subsequently to Cabral's discovery, from the quantity of the red wood abounding there.

The first known " Brasilium," or "Brésil," would be the Indian variety (Cæsalpinia Sappan), introduced into Europe, most probably, by the Venetians or Genoese, and obtained by them from the Levant, brought there by caravans, or by the Persian and Arabian Gulfs.

" Campesche," or Campeachy wood, " Hæmatoxyllum Campechianum" (Linn.)

which are seen in the forests, that it is not possible to feel more. Next are met large level plains as far as the eye can see, with immense flocks of cattle, such as horses, mules, oxen, cows, sheep, and goats, which have pastures always fresh in every season, there being no winter, but an air very temperate, neither hot nor cold. It only rains twice in the year, but the dews are so heavy at night that the plants are sufficiently watered and nourished. Besides that, the whole of the country is ornamented with very fine rivers and streams, which traverse almost the whole of the kingdom, and which, for the greater part, are navigable for boats.

The land is very fertile, producing corn twice in the year, and in as great abundance as can be desired, and, whatever season it may be, there are always very good and fresh fruits on the trees ; for when one fruit arrives at maturity, others come, and thus succeed one to the other ; and the trees are never devoid of fruit, and are always green.

If the king of Spain would permit vines to be planted in this kingdom, they would fructify like the corn ; for I have seen grapes produced from a stock which some one had planted for pleasure, of which every grain was as large as a plum, as long as half the thumb, and much better than those of Spain.

But all the contentment that I had felt at the sight of things so agreeable, was but little in regard of that which I experienced when I beheld that beautiful city of Mechique, which I did not suppose to be so superbly built, with splendid temples, palaces, and fine houses ; and the streets well laid out, where are seen the large and handsome shops

A SILVE

de la facon quon le tire

etched by M. M.

ER MINE.

of the merchants, full of all sorts of very rich merchandise.

I think, as well as I can judge, that there are in the said city, twelve thousand to fifteen thousand Spanish inhabitants, and six times as many Indians, who are Christians, dwelling there, besides a great number of negro slaves.

This city is surrounded almost on every side by a lake, with the exception of one part, which may be about three hundred paces in length, which can be cut and fortified. On this side only is there anything to be feared, as on all the other sides it is more than a league to the borders of the lake, into which fall four great rivers from far inland, and navigable for boats. One is called the river of Terra-Firma; another the river of Chile; another the river of Cacou; and the fourth, the river of Mechique, in which great quantities of fish are caught, of the same kind as we have with us, and very good. Along this river are a great number of fine gardens, and much arable land, very fertile.

Two leagues from the said Mechique there are silver mines, which the king of Spain has farmed out for five millions of gold a year, and he has reserved also the right of employing a great number of slaves, to get from the said mines as much as he can, for his profit; and he draws besides the tenth part of all that the farmers get, so that these mines are a very good revenue to the said king of Spain.

A great quantity of cochineal is gathered in this country, which grows in the fields as peas do elsewhere. It comes from a fruit the size of a walnut which is full of seed within.[1]

[1] "Cactus Opuntia. The belief that the cochineal was the seed of

It is left to come to maturity until the said seeds are dry, and then it is cut like corn and beaten to have the seed, of which they sow again so as to have more. It is the king of Spain alone who has the said cochineal sown and collected; and the merchants must buy it of his appointed officers, for it is merchandise of high price, and is esteemed as gold and silver.

There is a tree in the said country which is cut like the vine, and from the place where it is cut there distils an oil, which is a kind of balm, called oil of canima, from the name of the tree which is so called.[1] This is a singular oil for all sorts of wounds and cuts, and for removing pains, principally of gout. The wood has the odour of fir-tree wood. An ounce of the said oil is worth and sells for two crowns.

There is another tree, which is called cacou,[2] the fruit of which is very good and useful for many things, and even serves for money among the Indians, who give sixty for one real; each fruit is of the size of a pine-seed, and of the same shape; but the shell is not so hard; the older it is the better; and to buy provisions, such as bread, meat, fish, or herbs, this money may serve for five or six objects. Merchandise for provision can only be procured with it from the Indians, as

a plant, was prevalent for a very long period after the conquest of Mexico. In a drawing which Champlain gives of the plant, the " seeds" are shown exactly as the insects fix and feed on the leaves. The jealousy of the Spanish government, and the severe monopoly of this production, prevented the true nature and mode of propagation from being known, and gave rise to a variety of fables and conjectures.

[1] I am at a loss to find what tree it is that Champlain designates thus, unless it is " Canica"—Myrtus pimenta.

[2] The brown cacao (Linn.)

it is not current among the Spaniards, nor to buy often other merchandise than fruits. When this fruit is desired to be made use of, it is reduced to powder, then a paste is made, which is steeped in hot water, in which honey, which comes from the same tree, is mixed, and a little spice; then the whole being boiled together, it is drunk in the morning, warm, as our sailors drink brandy, and they find themselves so well after having drunk of it, that they can pass a whole day without eating or having great appetite.[1]

This tree bears numbers of thorns, which are very pointed; and when they are torn off, a thread comes from the bark of the said tree, which they spin as fine as they please; and with this thorn, and the thread which is attached to it, they can sew as well as with a needle and other thread. The Indians make very good, fine, and delicate thread of it, and nevertheless so strong, that a man cannot break two fibres of it together, although they may be as fine as hairs; the pound of this thread, called thread of Pitte[2], is worth in Spain, eight crowns, and with it, lace, and other valuable

[1] The supporting and stimulating properties of chocolate were discovered very early, and were particularly valuable in a country where the animal food gave but little nourishment. Gage says, that " Three or four hours after a repast of three or four dishes of beef, kid, turkey, and other game, his and company's stomachs were overcome with weakness and ready to faint, so that they were obliged to support and fortify them with a glass of chocolate," etc. This " strangeness" was attributed to the little nourishment in the meats, although in appearance as fine as those of Europe, owing to the extreme dryness of the pasturage.

[2] Champlain has here evidently the description of the cacao tree and the " Metl," or Maguey (Aloes Pitta, Aloes disticha, Agave Americana), to which nearly all the latter part of his description applies, save the " leaf like that of an olive tree."

works are made. From the bark of this tree vinegar is made, as strong as that from wine ; and taking the heart of this tree, and pressing it, there comes out very good honey : then drying the pith thus pressed in the sun, it serves to light fires. Moreover, in pressing the leaves of this tree, which are like those of the olive tree, there proceeds from them a juice, of which the Indians make a beverage. This tree is of the size of an olive tree.

I have before spoken of a tree which is called Gouiave,[1] which grows very commonly in this country, and bears a fruit also called Gouiave, of the size of an apple of Capendu,[2] of a yellow colour, and the inside like to that of green figs ; the juice is pretty good.

This fruit has the property, that if a person should have a flux of the belly, and should eat of the said fruit, without the skin, he would be cured in two hours ; and on the contrary, if a man be constipated, and eat the skin only, without the inside of the fruit, it would incontinently loosen his bowels, without need of other medicines.

There is also another fruit called Accoiates,[3] of the size of

---

[1] "Psidium" (Linn.)   "Sa qualité est de resserrer le ventre, estant mangé vert, dont aussi plusieurs s'en servent contre le flux de sang; mais estant mangé meur il a un effet tout contraire."—De Rochefort, *Hist. des Antilles*, etc., 1658.

[2] A kind of apple common in Normandy, in the "Pays de Caux" more particularly.

[3] "*Ahuacahuitl*," native name, by corruption called "Aguacat"; by the Spaniards, "Avorat," "Avogade," and "Avocat"—the Avogada pear.

"Shaped like a pear, sometimes like a lime, green without, green and white within, with a large kernel in the middle. It is eaten cooked or raw, with salt. All travellers agree that no fruit in Europe can compare with it."—Clusius.

Acoyates

fleur

large winter pears, very green outside : and when the skin is taken off, a very thick flesh is found, which is eaten with salt, and has the taste of kernels or green walnuts ; there is a stone in it, of the size of a walnut, of which the inside is bitter. The tree (branch) on which grows the said fruit, is here figured, together with the fruit.

Also there is a fruit, which is called Algarobe,[1] of the size of plums of Apt, and as long as bean-pods ; the shell of it is harder than that of cassia, and is of a chesnut colour ; a small fruit like a large green bean is found in it, which has a kernel, and is very good.

I saw also another fruit called Carreau, of the size of the first :[2] the skin is very tender, and of an orange colour ; the inside is red as blood, and the flesh like that of plums ; it

---

[1] Algaroba, or Algarova, the name given by the Spaniards to some species of acacia of the New World, from their resemblance to the algarobe, caroubier, St. John's bean, or carob tree, of which the pods form excellent food for cattle.

[2] The fruit of a variety of Cactus Opuntia—the "Nuchtli" of the Mexicans, and called "Raquette" by the French, from the shape of the leaves. "Ce que nos François appellent Raquette à cause de la figure de ses feuilles : sur quelques unes de ces feuilles, longues et herissées, croist un fruit de la grosseur d'une prune-datte ; quand il est meur, il est rouge dedans, et dehors comme de vermillon. Il a cette propriété, qu'il teint l'urine en couleur de sang aussi tost qu'on en a mangé, de sorte que ceux qui ne savent pas ce secret, craignent de s'estre rompu une veine, et il s'en est trouvé qui, aians apperceu ce changement, se sont mis au lit, et ont creu estre dangereusement malades."—De Rochefort, *Voyage aux Antilles*, etc., 1658.

This should be the same fruit of which Gage writes (1625-26) : "There is another sort of this fruit, 'Nuchtli,' which is red, and is not esteemed as the others, although not of bad taste, but on account of its staining with the colour of blood, not only the mouth and the linen of him who eats it, but also his urine."

stains where it touches, like mulberries: the taste is very good, and it is said to be excellent for curing the bite of venomous creatures.

There is also another fruit, which is named Serolles,[1] of the size of the plum, very yellow, and has the taste of muscatel pears.

I have also spoken of a tree named Palmiste.[2] It is twenty paces in height, and as large round as a man; nevertheless it is so tender, that with a good sword-stroke, it can be cut quite through, because the outside is as soft as a cabbage, and the inside full of marrowy-pith, which is very good, and firmer than the rest of the tree: it has the taste of sugar, as sweet, and better. The Indians make a drink of it, mixed with water, which is very good.

I saw also another fruit, called Cocques, of the size of an Indian nut,[3] which has a figure approaching to that of a man's head: for there are two holes which represent the two eyes, and that which advances between the two holes appears as the nose, underneath which there is a rather wide hole, which may be taken for the mouth, and the upper part of the said fruit is all frizzled, like curly hair; from the aforesaid holes issues a water, which is used as a medicine. When first plucked, this fruit is not good to eat;

---

[1] From the Spanish "Ciruela"—plum.

[2] In Champlain's time only two varieties of palm were known (save the cocoa-nut tree, which was called "palm" *par excellence*), the "Palmiste franc, or cabbage palm—Areca oleracea (Linn.); and the "Palmiste épineuse," or thorny palm—Areca spinosa (Linn.)

[3] "Cocos lapidea" of Gaertner, the fruit of which is smaller than the common cocoa-nut, and of which small vases, cups, etc., are made.

they let it dry, and make like little cups and bottles of it, as of Indian nuts, which come from the palm.

As I have spoken of the palm,[1] although it is a tree sufficiently common, I will here represent it. It is one of the highest and straightest trees that can be seen; its fruit, which is called " Indian nut," grows quite on the top of the tree, and is as large as the head of a man; and there is a thick green bark on the said nut, which bark being removed, the nut is found, about the size of two fists; that which is inside is very good to eat, and has the taste of young walnuts; there comes from it a water, which serves as a cosmetic for the ladies.[2]

There is another fruit called " Plante,"[3] of which the tree may be twenty or twenty-five feet high, which has a leaf so large, that a man might cover himself with it. There grows a root from the said tree, on which are a quantity of the " plantes," each of which is as thick as the arm, and a foot and a half long, of a yellow and green colour, of very good taste, and so wholesome, that a man can eat as much as he likes, without its doing any harm.

The Indians use a kind of corn which they call " Mamaix" (maize), which is of the size of a pea, yellow and red: and when they wish to eat it, they take a stone, hollowed like a mortar, and another, round, in the shape of a pestle: and after the said corn has been steeped for an hour, they grind

[1] Cocos nucifera.

[2] " C'est cette eau qui entre ses autres vertus, a la propriété d'effacer toutes les rides du visage, et de lui donner une couleur blanche et vermeille pourveu qu'on l'en lave aussi-tost que le fruit est tombé de l'arbre."—De Rochefort. [3] Plaintain-tree—Banana.

and reduce it to flour in the said stone; then they knead
and bake it in this manner. They take a plate of iron, or of
stone, which they heat on the fire : and when quite hot, they
take their paste, and spread it upon the plate rather thin,
like tart-paste ; and having thus cooked it, they eat it while
hot, for it is good for nothing, cold, or kept.

They have also another root, which they name Cassave,
which they use for making bread : but if any one should eat
of it, unprepared, he would die.

There is a gum called Copal,[1] which proceeds from a tree,
which is like the pine-tree : this gum is very good for gout
and pains.

There is also a root which is named patate, and which
they cook like pears at the fire :[2] it has a taste similar to
that of chesnuts.

In the said country, there are numbers of melons of
strange size, which are very good; the flesh is quite orange-
colour ; and there is another sort, of which the flesh is white,
but they are not of such good flavour as the others. There
are also quantities of cucumbers, very good; artichokes,
good lettuces, like those called with us " romaines," cab-

---

[1] Rhus Copallinum (Linn.) The Mexicans gave the name of "copal,"
to all resins and odoriferous gums. The "copal," par excellence, is a
white and transparent resin, which flows from a tree whose leaves resemble those of the oak, but longer ; this tree is called "copal-qua-
huitl, or tree which bears the copal ; they have also the "copal-qua-
huitl-petlahuae," whose leaves are the largest of the species, and like
those of the sumach. The "copal-quauhxiotl," with long and narrow
leaves ; the "tepecopulli-qua-huitl," or copal of the mountains, whose
resin is like the incense of the old world, called by the Spaniards,
" incienso de las Indias," and some other inferior kinds.

[2] Batatas—sweet potatoe, yam.

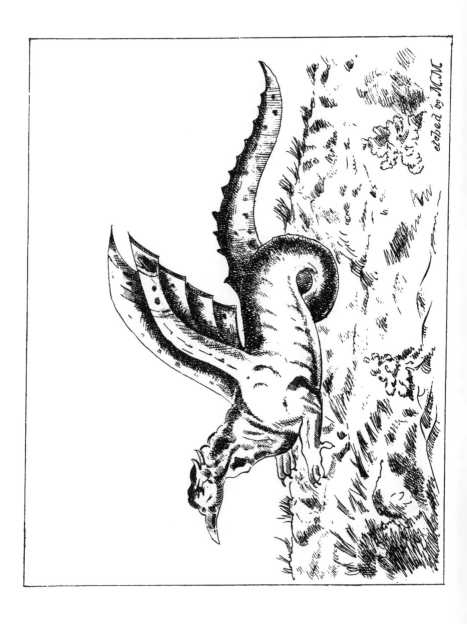

etched by M.M.

bages, and numerous other kitchen herbs; also pumpkins, which have red flesh, like the melons.

There are also apples, which are not very good, and pears, of tolerably good taste, which grow there naturally. I think that if any one would take the trouble to plant these good fruit trees in our climate, they would succeed very well.

Throughout New Spain, there is a kind of snake,[1] which is of the length of a pike, and as thick as the arm; the head as large as a hen's egg, on which they have two plumes; at the end of the tail they have a rattle, which makes a noise as they glide along. They are very dangerous with their teeth, and with their tail; nevertheless, the Indians eat them, after having taken away the two extremities.

There are also dragons of strange figure, having the head approaching to that of an eagle, the wings like those of a bat, the body like a lizard, and has only two rather large feet; the tail somewhat scaly, and it is as large as a sheep; they are not dangerous, and do no harm to any body, though to see them, you would say the contrary.

I have seen a lizard of such strange size, that if it had been related to me by another, I should not have believed it. I assure you that they are as large as a quarter pipe. They are like those that we see here, as to their form; their colour is greenish-brown, and greenish-yellow under the belly: they run very fast, and hiss in running; they are not mischievous to men, although they do not fly from them

[1] Champlain clearly means the rattle-snake (Crotulus), but seems to have confounded it with the horned snake, from the "plumes" on the head.

unless pursued. The Indians eat them, and find them very good.[1]

I have also many times seen in that country, animals that they call caymans, which are, as I believe, a kind of crocodile,[2] and so large, that certain of the said caymans are twenty-five and thirty feet in length, and are very dangerous; for if they should find a man unawares, without doubt they would devour him. They are of a whitish-yellow colour under the belly, the back armed with strong scales of brownish-green colour, having the head very long, and the teeth strangely sharp; the mouth very wide, the eyes red, and very flaming; on the head there is a sort of crown; they have four very short legs, the body of the size of a barrel. There are also smaller ones. From beneath the hind thighs excellent musk is procured. They live in the lakes and marshes, and in the fresh-water rivers. The Indians eat them.

I have also seen tortoises of marvellous size, such that two horses would have difficulty in dragging one of them; and there are some so large that, in the shell which covers them, three men could place themselves and float as in a boat. They are fished in the sea. The flesh of them is very

---

[1] Probably "Lacerta Iguana" (Linn.), some of which grow to a great size. The flesh was considered a delicacy by the Indians and by many Europeans, but eating of it too frequently was supposed to occasion a wasting of the body. De Rochefort says : "On ne conseille néanmoins d'en manger souvent à cause qu'elle dessêche trop le corps et lui fait perdre tout son embonpoint."—*Hist. Nat. et Morale des Antilles.*

[2] In another room there were great earthen vessels, some filled with water, others with earth, in which were snakes as big as a man's thigh ; and crocodiles, which they call caymans, as thick as a man's thigh."— Gage, *Description of the Palace of Montezuma.*

good and resembles beef. They are in great quantity in all the Indies, and they are often seen going to feed in the woods.

There are also numbers of tigers,[1] of the skin of which great care is taken. They do not attack unless pursued.

There are also to be seen in the said country, some civettes,[2] which come from Peru, where there are quantities.

There comes from Peru to New Spain a certain kind of sheep which, like horses, carry burthens of more than four hundred pounds for days together. They are of the size of an ass; the neck very long, the head middling; the wool very long, and which more resembles hair like that of a goat than wool. They have not horns like our sheep, and are very good to eat, but their flesh is not so delicate as that of our sheep.[3]

The country is much peopled with stags and hinds, roe-bucks, wild boars, foxes, hares, rabbits, and other animals which we have in our parts, and from which they are not at all different.

There is a kind of little animal of the size of prawns, which fly by night, and make such light in the air that one would say that they were so many little candles. If a man had three or four of these little creatures, which are not larger than a filbert, he could read as well at night as with a wax light.[4]

In the woods and in the plains are to be found numbers

[1] Tigris Americana (Linn.)—Jaguar.
[2] Viverra civetta (Linn.)—the Gato de Algalia of the Spaniards.
[3] The Llama, or Vicuña.
[4] The Lantern fly—Fulgora suternaria (Linn.)

of crabs,¹ like to those which are found in the sea, and are also as common on land as in the sea elsewhere.

There is another small kind of animal like a crawfish, excepting that they have the hinder parts devoid of shell; but they have this property—of seeking the empty shells of snails and lodging therein the part which is uncovered, dragging the shell always after them, and are only to be dislodged by force.² The fishermen collect these little beasts in the woods, and make use of them for fishing; and when they wish to catch fish, having taken the little animals from the shell, they attach them by the middle of the body to their lines instead of hooks, then throw them into the sea, and when the fish think to swallow them, they seize the fish with their two powerful claws and will not let them go; and by these means, the fishermen catch fish of the weight even of five or six pounds.

I have seen a bird which is named " pacho del ciello,"³ that is to say, bird of the heavens, which name is given to it because it is continually in the air without ever coming to the earth till it falls dead.   It is of the size of a sparrow. Its head is very small, the beak short; part of the body greenish-brown, the rest somewhat red.   It has a tail of

¹ " Gecarcinus," Cancer ruricolor (Linn)—land crab.

² The hermit-lobster, " pagurus streblany," (Leach) ; " pagurus Bernardus (Fabricius) ; "cancellus marinus et terrestris."   Bernard l'hermite of the French ; caracol soldada of the Spaniards.

³ Pacho del ciello.—" Paradisia."—Bird of Paradise. The belief was long prevalent that these birds lived constantly in the air, having no feet.   The specimens sent to Europe had seldom the legs and feet attached, the body and tail being only used as an aigrette or plume ; hence the idea of their not having any feet.

AN INDIAN

FEAST.

more than two feet in length, almost like an aigrette, and singularly large. With respect to the body, it has no feet. It is said that the female lays one egg only on the back of the male, by whose heat the said egg is hatched, and when the bird has left the shell, it remains in the air, in which it lives like the rest of its kind. I have only seen one, which our general bought for one hundred and fifty crowns. They are to be caught towards the coast of Chile, which is a great extent of Terra-Firma, extending from Peru as far as the Straits of Magellan, which the Spaniards are examining, and are at war with the savages of the country, where, it is said, mines of gold and silver are found.

I think it not out of place here to say that ebony wood comes from a very high tree, like to the oak : the outside of the bark is whitish and the heart very black.

The Brésil is a tree, very large compared with the ebony tree, of the same height, but it is not so hard ; the said Brésil bears a kind of nut, which grows to about the size of gall-nuts which come on elm trees.

After having spoken of the trees, plants, and animals, I must give a short account of the Indians, their nature, manners, and belief. The greater number of the said Indians, who are not under the domination of the Spaniards, adore the moon as their Deity, and when they desire to perform their ceremonies, they assemble, great and small, in the middle of their villages, and place themselves in a circle ; those who have anything to eat, bring it, and they put all the provisions together in the midst of them and make the best cheer possible. After they are well satisfied, they all take each other by the hand, and begin dancing with loud and strange cries, their song having no order or connexion. After they have well sung and danced, they place themselves with their faces to the earth, and all at once, they altogether begin to cry out and weep, saying, "Oh! powerful and bright moon, grant that we may conquer our enemies, and may eat them, that we may not fall into their hands; and that, dying, we may go and rejoice with our relatives." After having made this prayer, they rise and set about dancing in a round; and their feasts last thus, dancing, singing, and praying, about six hours. This is what I have learned about the ceremonies and belief of these poor people, deprived of reason, whom I have here figured.

As for the other Indians who are under the dominion of the king of Spain, if he did not take some order about them, they would be as barbarous in their belief as the others. At the commencement of his conquests, he had established the Inquisition among them, and made slaves of or caused them to die cruelly in such great numbers, that the sole recital would cause pity. This evil treatment was the reason that the poor Indians, for very apprehension, fled to the mountains in desperation, and as many Spaniards as they caught they ate them; and on that account the said Spaniards were constrained to take away the Inquisition, and allow them personal liberty, granting them a more mild and tolerable rule of life, to bring them to the knowledge of God and the belief of the holy church; for if they had continued still to chastise them according to the rigor of the said Inquisition, they would have caused them all to die by fire.

BURNING

INDIANS.

The system that is now used is, that in every estance (estancia), which are like our villages, there is a priest who regularly instructs them, the said priest having a list of the names and surnames of all the Indians who inhabit the village under his charge.

There is also an Indian, who is as the fiscal of the village,[1] and he has another and similar list; and on the Sunday, when the priest wishes to say mass, all the said Indians are obliged to present themselves to hear it; and before the priest begins the mass, he takes his list, and calls them all by their names and surnames; and should any of them be absent, he is marked upon the list, and the mass being said, the priest charges the Indian who serves as fiscal, to inquire privately where the defaulters are, and to bring them to the church; in which, being brought before the priest, he asks them the reason why they did not come to the divine service, for which they allege some excuse, if they can find any; and if the excuses are not found to be true or reasonable, the said priest orders the fiscal to give the said defaulters thirty or forty blows with a stick, outside the church, and before all the people.

This is the system which is maintained to keep them in religion, in which they remain, partly from fear of being

[1] Indian Fiscal. "According to the size of the village, the church will have a certain number of singers, of trumpeters and players of the hautbois, over whom the priest appoints a certain officer, whom they call the fiscal, who walks before them with a white staff in his hand, having a cross of silver at the top, to show that he is an officer of the church. On the Sundays and feast days he is obliged to assemble the young men and girls at the church, before and after the service."— Gage's *Voyage*.

beaten. It is nevertheless true, that if they have some just reason which prevents them coming to the mass, they are excused.

All these Indians are of a very melancholy humour, but have nevertheless very quick intelligence, and understand in a short time, whatever may be shewn to them, and do not become irritated, whatever action or abuse may be done or said to them. I have figured in this page and the next, what may well represent that which I have discoursed above.

The greater part of these Indians have strange habitations, and are without any fixed residence; for they have a kind of caravan or cart, which is covered with the bark of trees, and drawn by horses, mules or oxen; they have their wives and children in the said caravans, and remain a month or two in one spot, and then remove to another, and are thus continually wandering about the country.

There is another class of Indians who build their dwellings and live in certain villages which belong to nobles or merchants, and cultivate the soil.

Now to return to the discourse of my voyage.

After having remained an entire month at Mechique, I returned to St. Jean de Luz, at which place I embarked in a patache, for Porto-bello, from which it is four or five hundred leagues. We were three weeks at sea before arriving at the said Porto-bello, when I found a great change of country; for, instead of the very good and fertile land, which I had seen in New Spain, as I have related above, I found a very bad country; this place of Porto-bello being the

PUNISHMENT OF THE INDIANS

FOR NOT ATTENDING CHURCH.

most evil and pitiful residence in the world. It rains there almost always, and if the rain ceases for an hour, the heat is so great, that the water becomes quite infected, and renders the air contagious, so that the greater part of the newly arrived soldiers and mariners die. The country is very mountainous, covered with forests of fir, in which there are such quantities of monkeys, that it is wonderful to behold. Nevertheless, the said harbour of Porto-bello is very good ; there are two castles at the entrance, which are tolerably strong, where there are three hundred soldiers in garrison. Adjoining the said port, where the fortresses are, there is another, which is not at all commanded by them, and where an army might land safely. The king of Spain esteems this port a place of consequence, being near to Peru, there being only seventeen leagues to Panama, which is on the south coast.

This port of Panama, which is on the sea of the (south), is very good; there is good anchorage, and the town is very mercantile.

In this place of Panama is collected all the gold and silver which comes from Peru, and where it is embarked, with other riches, upon a little river, which rises in the mountains, and descends to Porto-bello; which river is four leagues from Panama, from whence all the gold, silver, and merchandise must be conveyed on mules : and being embarked on the said river, there are but eighteen leagues to Porto-bello.

One may judge that, if the four leagues of land which there are from Panama to this river were cut through, one might pass from the south sea to the ocean on the other side, and thus shorten the route by more than fifteen hundred leagues;[1] and from Panama to the Straits of Magellan, would be an island, and from Panama to the New-foundlands would be another island, so that the whole of America would be in two islands.

If an enemy of the king of Spain should hold the said Porto-bello, he could prevent any thing leaving Peru, except with great difficulty and risk, and at more expense than profit. Drac[2] went to the said Porto-bello, in order to surprise it, but he failed in his enterprise, having been discovered; in consequence of which, he died from disappointment, and ordered, in dying, that they should put him in a coffin of lead, and throw him into the sea, between an island and the said Porto-bello.

Having remained a month at the said Porto-bello, I re-

[1] Isthmus of Panama. The junction of the Atlantic and Pacific oceans, through the Isthmus of Panama, is not therefore by any means a modern idea. Champlain has, perhaps, the merit of being the first to promulgate it.

[2] Sir Francis Drake, after his unsuccessful attempt on Porto-rico, pursued his voyage to Nombre-de-Dios, where, having landed his men, he attempted to pass forward to Panama with a view of plundering that place, or if he found such a scheme practicable, of keeping and fortifying it, but he met not with the same facility which had attended his first enterprises in those parts. The Spaniards had fortified the passes, and stationed troops in the woods, who so infested the English with continual alarms and skirmishes, that they were obliged to return without effecting anything. Drake himself, from the intemperance of the climate, the fatigues of his journey and the vexation of his disappointment, was seized with a distemper of which he soon after died. (See Hume's " Hist. of England," ann. 1597. Drake died on the 30th of December, 1596, old style, (9th of January, 1597, MS.,) and his body was disposed of in the manner mentioned by Champlain.

turned to St. Jean de Luz, where we sojourned fifteen days, waiting while our ships were careened, to go to the Havanna, to the rendezvous of the armies and fleets; and for that purpose, having left the said St. Jean de Luz, when we were twenty leagues at sea, a hurricane took us with such fury, with a north wind, that we thought all was lost, and were so separated one from the other, that we could only rally at the Havanna. On the other hand, our ship made so much water, that we thought we could not avoid the peril; for if we took half an hour's repose, without pumping out the water, we were obliged to work for two hours without ceasing; and had we not met with a patache, which set us in our route again, we should have been lost on the coast of Campesche.

On this coast of Campesche, there are quantities of salt, which is made and procured without artificial means, by reservoirs of water, which remain after the high tides, where it crystallizes in the sun.

Our pilot had lost all knowledge of the navigation, but the grace of God sent us this meeting with the patache.

Arrived at the Havanna, we found our general, but our admiral had not yet arrived, which made us think that he was lost; however, he came in soon after, with the remainder of the ships. Eighteen days after our arrival, I embarked in a vessel which was going to Cartagena, and we were fifteen days making the voyage. This place is a good port, where there is a fine entrance, sheltered from all winds, save from the north-north-west, which blows into the harbour, in which there are three islands. The king of Spain keeps two galleys here. The said place is in the country called terra-firma, which is very good, very fertile, as well in corn and fruits as in other things necessary to life; but not in such abundance as in New Spain; but in recompense, there is a greater quantity of silver drawn from the said country of terra-firma.

I remained a month and a half at the town of Cartagena, and took a portrait of the town and of the harbour.

Leaving the said port of Cartagena, I returned to the Havanna, to meet our general, who gave me a very good reception, having visited by his command the places where I had been.

The said port of Havanna is one of the finest that I have seen in all the Indies. The entrance is very narrow, very good, and well furnished with all that is necessary to defend it; and from one fort to the other there is an iron chain, which traverses the entry of the port. The garrison of the said fortresses consists of six hundred soldiers; that is to say, in one, named the Moro, on the eastern side, four hundred; and in the other fort, which is called the new fort, and is in the town, two hundred. Inside the said harbour there is a bay, which is more than six leagues round, being more than one league wide, where in every part ships can anchor in three, four, six, eight, ten, fifteen, and sixteen fathoms water, and a great number of vessels can remain there; the town is very good and mercantile.

The island, in which are the fort and city of Havanna, is called Cuba, and is very mountainous; there are no mines of gold or silver, but many mines of metal, of which pieces of artillery are made for the town of Havanna.

Neither corn nor wine grows on the said island; that which is consumed comes from New Spain, so that sometimes they are very dear.

In this island there are quantities of very good fruits; among others one which is called pines,[1] which perfectly resembles in shape the pine (cones) with us. The skin is removed, then it is cut in half like apples; it has a very good taste, and is very sweet, like sugar.

There is abundance of cattle, such as oxen, cows, and pigs, which are better meat than any other in this country, or in all the Indies. They keep a great number of oxen, more to have the hides than the flesh. To take them, negroes go on horseback after these oxen, and with astes,[2] at the end of which is a very sharp crescent, cut the hamstrings of the oxen, which are immediately skinned, and the flesh so soon consumed, that, twenty-four hours after, none can be perceived, being devoured by great numbers of wild dogs and other animals which inhabit this country.

We were four months at the Havanna, and leaving it with the whole fleet of the Indies, which had assembled there from all parts, we proceeded to pass the channel of Bahan (Bahama), which is a passage of consequence, and which must necessarily be passed in returning from the Indies. On one side of the said passage, to the north, lies the land of Florida, and on the other the Havanna. The sea flows

[1] Pine-apple. Piña de Indias (Span.) anana.
[2] Hasta (Lat.), lance or pole.

7

into the said channel with great impetuosity. This channel
is eighty leagues in length, and in width eight leagues, as it
is figured hereafter, together with the land of Florida, at
least such part of the coast as can be seen.

On quitting the said channel we came near to Bermuda,
a mountainous island which it is difficult to approach on
account of the dangers that surround it. It almost always
rains there, and thunders so often, that it seems as if heaven
and earth were about to come together. The sea is very
tempestuous around the said island, and the waves high as
mountains.[1]

Having passed the traverse of the said island, we saw
such quantities of flying-fish that it was marvellous.[2] We
took some which fell on board our ship. They have the
shape like that of a herring; the fins much larger, and are
very good to eat.

There are certain fish as large as barrels, which are called
" tribons,"[3] which follow the flying-fish to eat them; and
when the flying fish find that they cannot otherwise avoid
them, they spring from the water and fly about five hundred
paces, and by this means they save themselves from the said
" tribon."

---

[1] Bermuda. " The still vexed Bermoothes." Gage was nearly wrecked
on the rocks of Bermuda. He says, " The Spaniards, instead of thanking
God for having saved them from that peril, began to curse the English
who inhabited the island, saying that they had enchanted it, and all the
others in the neighbourhood, and that, by means of the devil, they
caused storms to arise whenever a Spanish fleet passed."

[2] Flying fish. Exocetus volitans (Linn.)

[3] Tiburon (Span.) Shark, probably confounded with the bonito,
which with the dorade (sparus aurata) is the mortal enemy of the
flying-fish.

I must also say that on the south-south-east side of the said channel of Bahan is seen the island of St. Domingo, of which I have before spoken, which is very fine and commercial in hides, ginger, and casse-tabac, which is otherwise called petun,[1] or the queen's herb, which is dried and then made into little cakes. Sailors, even the English, and other persons use it, and take the smoke of it in imitation of the savages.

Although I have before represented the island of St. Domingo, I will nevertheless figure the coast towards the channel of Bahan.

I have spoken above of the land of Florida; I will also say that it is one of the best lands that can be desired; very fertile if it were cultivated, but the king of Spain does not care for it because there are no mines of gold or silver. There are great numbers of savages, who make war against the Spaniards, who have a fort on a point of the said land, where there is a harbour. The land is low, and for the most part very agreeable.

Four days after passing Bermuda we had such a great tempest, that the whole of our armament was more than six days without being able to keep together. After the six days had passed, the weather becoming finer and the sea more tranquil, we all reassembled, and had the wind favourable till we perceived the Açores. The island of Terceira is shown here.

[1] Most likely "canasse," or canaster tobacco, or petun-nicotiana tabacum (Linn.) Nicot, who first introduced tobacco in France, called it "herbe à la reine," or the queen's herb. The term "petuner" was often used formerly instead of "fumer," to smoke. "Ils" (the Indians) "ne font du feu que pour petuner."—Champlain's *Voyages en Nouvelle France*, 1632.

All vessels returning from the Indies must of necessity approach the said islands of Açores to take their observations, otherwise they could not with surety finish their route.

Having passed the isles of Açores, we came in sight of Cape St. Vincent, where we captured two English ships which were armed for war; and we took them to the river of Seville from whence we had departed, and which was the termination of our voyage; which had occupied, since our leaving the river of Seville, as well on sea as on land, two (three) years and two months.

FINIS.

For EU product safety concerns, contact us at Calle de José Abascal, 56–1°,
28003 Madrid, Spain or eugpsr@cambridge.org.

www.ingramcontent.com/pod-product-compliance
Ingram Content Group UK Ltd.
Pitfield, Milton Keynes, MK11 3LW, UK
UKHW012346130625
459647UK00009B/560